The Rise and Fall of Western Tanks

Volume I

1855-1939

Bruce Oliver Newsome, Ph.D.

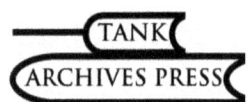

The Rise and Fall of Western Tanks
Volume I
1855-1939

by Bruce Oliver Newsome, Ph.D.
www.BruceNewsome.com

Sign up for bonus chapters, photographs, and videos.

Published by: Tank Archives Press,
PO Box 181802, Coronado, California 92178,
United States of America

Copyright © 2021 Tank Archives Press

All rights reserved. No part of this publication may be reproduced or stored in a retrieval system or transmitted, in any form or by any means, electronic, mechanical, photocopying, recording or otherwise, without prior permission in writing from Tank Archives Press.

HIS027090	HISTORY / Military / World War I
HIS027100	HISTORY / Military / World War II
HIS027240	HISTORY / Military / Vehicles
NHWR5	First World War
NHWR7	Second World War
NHWL	Modern warfare
JWMV	Military vehicles

ISBN: 978-1-951171-05-6
2nd edition

Acknowledgements

The author wishes to thank:

- Rob Cogan, Curator, US Armor and Cavalry Collection
- John Dethlefsen, interned researcher
- Maiqi Ding, University of Chiacgo
- David Fletcher, Historian, The Tank Museum
- Charlotte Greenberg, University of Chicago
- Jonathan Holt, Archives Assistant, Tank Museum
- Richard E. Killblane, Historian, US Army Transportation Corps
- Danny Ma, University of California Berkeley
- Yurii Pasholok, independent armoured vehicle historian
- Sheldon Rogers, Archives Assistant, Tank Museum
- Taki, founder of http://www3.plala.or.jp/takihome.
- Katie Thompson, Archives Assistant, Tank Museum
- Stuart Wheeler, Archives Manager, Tank Museum
- David Willey, Curator, Tank Museum

All photographs are courtesy of: Bundesarchiv (Germany), US Army Center for Military History, Museo Storico Italiano della Guerra di Roverto (Italy), National Archives (US), Imperial War Museum, The Tank Museum (Britain), and Bruce Oliver Newsome, Ph.D..

CONTENTS

Tables and Graphs	4
Abbreviations	5
Introduction	7
Chapter 1: Why Britain was first with tanks	11
Britain's foundations	11
American and British tractors	14
Army gun tractors	16
Admiralty gun tractors	17
Admiralty bridgelayer	17
Armored Holts	19
Rollers	22
Army Holt tractors	23
Big wheel gunships and small wheel wagons	26
Wheeled trench enfilader	28
Tracked Self-Moving Cupola	30
Foster Trench Tractor	31
Track research	32
Consolidating efforts	35
Lingering big wheels	39
Lingering Self-Moving Cupolas	39
Number 1 Lincoln Machine (Little Willie)	43
Centipede (Big Willie)	44
Why was Britain first?	47
Chapter 2: Why the rest were next	51
France	51
Germany and Austro-Hungary	55
America	56
Russia	60
Italy	61
Dominions	62
Conclusion	62
Chapter 3: Why West was best, 1916-1918	65
British heavy tanks: mobility	65
British heavy tanks: lethality	67
British heavy tanks: survivability	69
British medium tanks	69
French tanks	70
German tanks	71
Italian tanks	76
American tanks	76

Chapter 4: Britain's rise and fall, 1919-1939		79
Rise		79
Fall		82
Realization		85
Revisionism		93
Chapter 5: French proliferation, 1919-1939		95
Super-Heavy and Heavy tanks		95
Light/Medium tanks		96
Light tanks		97
Chapter 6: American under-ambition, 1919-1939		105
Light tanks		105
Medium tanks		105
Realization		107
Chapter 7: Italian and Japanese exceptionalism		109
Italian tankettes		109
Italian light tanks		110
Italian medium tanks		111
Japanese medium tanks		112
Japanese light tanks		114
Chapter 8: Soviet, German, and Czech catch-up		117
Soviet tanks		117
German tanks		122
Czechoslovakian tanks		125
Chapter 9: Conclusion		127
Appendices: Dataset methodology and sources		130

TABLES & GRAPHS

Table 1:	Tractors tried or acquired by Western militaries, 1857-1915	20
Table 2:	British proposals for tanks, 1855-1915	24
Table 3:	Time taken to procure and deploy tanks during World War I	50
Table 4:	Tank acquisitions, economics, and politics during World War I	63
Graph 1:	Relative effectiveness of tanks piloted from 1916 to 1919	72
Graph 2:	Relative efficiency of tanks piloted from 1916 to 1919	73
Table 5:	Specifications and performance of platforms of World War I	77
Graph 3:	Relative effectiveness of tanks piloted in the 1920s	98
Graph 4:	Relative efficiency of tanks piloted in the 1920s	99
Graph 5:	Relative effectiveness of tanks piloted in the 1930s	102
Graph 6:	Relative efficiency of tanks pilots in the 1930s	103
Table 6:	Tank pilots, effectiveness, efficiency, by nationality, 1916-1939	126
Graph 7:	Average tank effectiveness, by nation, by period	126
Graph 8:	Average tank efficiency, by nation, by period	126

ABBREVIATIONS

ACIGS	Assistant Chief of the Imperial General Staff
AB	armored brigade
AD	armored division
AFHQ	Allied Force Headquarters
AFV	armoured fighting vehicle
a.k.a.	also known as
amn	ammunition
AP	armor-piercing; Associated Press
APC	armor-piercing, capped
APCBC	armor-piercing, capped, ballistic capped
APCR	armor-piercing, composite rigid
APDS	armor-piercing, discarding sabot
API	armor-piercing, incendiary
APT	armor-piercing, tracer
AT	anti-tank
Ausf.	*Ausführung* (mark or iteration)
bhp	brake horse-power
BAOR	British Army of the Rhine
BEF	British Expeditionary Force
BRAC	Brigader Royal Armoured Corps (a staff officer at field army echelon)
CC	Combat Command
CIGS	Chief of the Imperial General Staff
CIOS	Combined Intelligence Objectives Sub-Committee
cm	centimetres
CP	command post
CT	Combat Team
DA	Director of Artillery
DADME	Deputy Assistant Director of Mechanical Engineering
DAFV	Directorate of Armoured Fighting Vehicles
DCIGS	Deputy Chief of the Imperial General Staff
DDAFV(T)	Deputy Director of Armoured Fighting Vehicles Technology
DDGA	Deputy Director-General of Artillery
DDME	Deputy Director of Mechanical Engineering
DGA	Director-General of Artillery
DGAE	Director-General for Army Equipment
dm	decimetres
DME	Director of Mechanical Engineering
DMI	Directorate of Military Intelligence
DMO&I	Directorate of Military Operations and Intelligence
DRA	Director Royal Artillery
DRAC	Director Royal Armoured Corps
DSD	Director of Staff Duties
DTD	Department of Tank Design
FA	Field Artillery
FlaK	*Fliegerabwehrkanone* (anti-aircraft gun)
FO	(British) Foreign Office
fps	feet per second
ft.	feet
FVPE	(British) Fighting Vehicle Proving Establishment
G1	(American) branch of the staff responsible for personnel
G2	(American) branch of the staff responsible for intelligence
G3	(American) branch of the staff responsible for operations and training
G4	(American) branch of the staff responsible for logistics
GC&CS	(British) Government Code and Cypher School
GHQ	General Headquarters (usually field army or regional echelon)
HC	hollow charge (shaped charge)
HE	high-explosive
HEAT	high-explosive anti-tank (HC)

HET	high-explosive, tracer
hp	horse-power
HQ	headquarters
hrs.	hours (24-hour clock)
IC	in charge
in.	inch
IRTC	Inspector Royal Tank Corps
IWM	Imperial War Museum
JIC	(British) Joint Intelligence Sub-Comittee, Chiefs of Staff
km	kilometers
kmh or kph	kilometers per hour
KwK	*Kampfwagenkanone* (fighting vehicle gun)
L	length in calibers
lb.	pound
LHCMA	Liddell Hart Centre for Military Archives
m	metres
M	model
MC	military cross
MEC	(British Army) Middle East Command
MEW	Ministry for Economic Warfare
MG	machine-gun
MI	military intelligence
Mk.	mark
mm	millimetres
MP	Member of Parliament; Military Police
mph	miles per hour
MQ	machineable quality armour (also: RHA)
m/s	metres per second
nhp	nominal horsepower
OKW	*Oberkommando der Wehrmacht* (High Command of Armed Forces)
OR	other rank
PaK	*Panzerabwehrkanone* (anti-tank gun)
Panzer	*Panzerkampfwagen* (armoured fighting vehicle)
pdr	pounder (a gun; numerical prefix is nominal weight of projectile)
Pkw	*Personenkraftwagen* (personnel carrier)
Pz.Kfw./Pz.Kw.	*Panzerkampfwagen* (armoured fighting vehicle)
pr	pounder (see: pdr)
QF	quick firing
RA	Royal Artillery
RAC	Royal Armoured Corps
RACTM	Royal Armoured Corps Tank Museum, Bovington, Dorset, England
RAOC	Royal Army Ordnance Corps
RASC	Royal Army Service Corps
RE	Royal Engineers
REME	Royal Electrical and Mechanical Engineers
RHA	rolled homogenous armour; Royal Horse Artillery
RTC	Royal Tank Corps
RTR	Royal Tank Regiment
Sd.Kfz.	*Sonderkraftfahrzeug* (special purpose vehicle)
SHAEF	Supreme Headquarters Allied Expeditionary Force
SIS	(British) Secret Intelligence Service (MI6)
sq.	square
SS	steamship; *Schutzstaffel* (protection staff); Security Service (MI5)
StuG	*Sturmgeschütz* (assault vehicle)
StuK	*Sturmgeschützkanone* (assault vehicle gun)
STT	School of Tank Technology
SW	*Sturmwagen* (assault vehicle)
TD	Tank Destroyer
tk.	tank
TM	see: RACTM
UK	United Kingdom
US(A)	United States (of America)
WD	War Department
WO	War Office
WTSFF	Weapons Technical Staff Field Force
yds.	yards

INTRODUCTION

How did the most industrialized, wealthy, democratic countries lose their lead in tanks? This volume is the first to combine the methods of history and science to resolve a controversy that has endured for a century.

In both world wars, Western European, North American, and Australasian states were democratic, industrialized, and rich. They shared a dominant Western culture. They tended to ally with each other. Materially, their alliances overawed their enemies. Britain, France, and the United States (US) acquired the first, largest, and best tank forces of the First World War. They ended victorious. They remained dominant, despite peacetime turmoil.

In tanks, the Western great powers remained innovative in the 1920s, but were misguided by the 1930s. Worse, they were overtaken by the very states they tried to contain. The Western great powers were practically the sole architects of peacetime international institutions, laws, norms, and rules. Their international regime was meant to contain the losers of the First World War: Germany, Austria, Hungary, the new states born of their empires (such as Czechoslovakia), and a revolutionary communist Russian empire (eventually named as the Union of Soviet Socialist Republics; USSR). These states were late developers. However, during the 1930s, the USSR and Germany (eventually incorporating Austria and Czechoslovakia) developed the largest tank forces, reverse-engineered Western tanks, and innovated for themselves. They achieved quantitative and qualitative superiority despite less capital and smaller automotive industries. By then, they were strong autocracies, with a central- to eastern-European, anti-Western orientation.

In detail, Western tanks were curiously diverse and unbalanced. French, British, and US light and medium tanks prioritized speed. British infantry tanks and French heavy tanks prioritized survivability. Italy (one of the Western Allies of the Great War) switched to tankettes as replacements for tanks, after most other states realized tankettes as carriers and tractors. Japan (which also had sided with the West in the Great War) invested in heavy-mediums, before switching to lights.

During the Second World War (the focus of Volume II in this series), Western states innovated but never caught up with Germany and the USSR. They developed more new base models and variants of old models than their enemies, without satisfying user requirements. They ended the war qualitatively inferior in tanks, and quantitatively inferior in units and formations, despite producing more types of tank. The USSR produced the most tanks and boasted superior types than the next most productive country (the US). If the war had continued into 1946, German and Soviet tanks still would have been better developed than Western tanks. With Germany defeated, the USSR maintained its lead into the Cold War.

Western soldiers complained about their tanks, while propagandists pretended otherwise. Governments deferred official inquiry until after the emergency, then forgot their promises. Politicians spun the story to avoid blame or monopolize credit, as convenient. Official historians ignored the record. Private historians lazily and nationalistically followed their respective official histories. Germany's defeat, and hostility towards the Soviet bloc, did not incentivize the West to admit its failings. Popular culture rightly celebrated ultimate victory, and the West's superior naval and air forces, but not tanks.

Realism about the failings of Western tanks declined from the mid-1990s, with the rise of revisionist fields and media. Television, the internet, and social media are often said to democratize knowledge, but really they popularize consensus. Almost everything said on tanks in the public domain relies on hearsay. One would hope for the experts to provide the virtues, but the academic and defense communities are producing fewer experts. The consensus is increasingly agenda-driven, rather than evidence-based. Social scientists focus on the sociology, politics, and economics. Historians retell the personalities and battles. The technologies appear as a few qualitative judgments ("weak," "powerful," "unreliable") and quantitative measures (gun caliber, armor thickness, and speed). Rarely are these data sourced or cited. Recent histories regress to the propaganda, politics, and nationalism of the time. Even the fact of the Western tank scandal has been denied.

THE RISE AND FALL OF WESTERN TANKS is not about how tanks were used, how forces were structured, or how forces were employed, which are worthy topics for subsequent books. This series focuses on tanks as types. You will see the data and read the judgments direct from the developers and users themselves, in real time. Most of these data and quotes were ignored by official historians, and subsequently archived without reference to the tanks they describe.

In these volumes, you will see more than 400 photographs and dozens of tables and graphs. You will see analysis of an unprecedented dataset of tank attributes, providing quantitative evidence to counter the hearsay and comfortable myths. This dataset covers more than 500 tank types, up to 22 attributes per tank, 40 years (1916-1955), and 9 national producers (USA, Canada, Britain, France, Germany, Czechoslovakia, Italy, Russia/Soviet Union, Japan).

This first volume follows the birth of tanks, from the first tractors and imagined military vehicles of the 1850s, through the first tanks of the First World War and the developments of the 1920s and 1930s, up to the Second World War in 1939.

The first chapter explains the technological foundations for tanks since the 1850s, and why Britain was first to put them together. The second chapter explains the states that followed Britain in deploying tanks during the Great War. The third chapter shows that Western tanks were the best of those deployed by 1918, and reveals the neglected German designs that would have shocked the West if the war had continued into 1919. The fourth chapter reveals Britain's further inventiveness in the 1920s, but also its trend to light weight, until belated revival in the late 1930s. The fifth chapter tells of France's leadership in the 1920s, before its proliferation of light tanks. The sixth chapter tells how America tried impressive technologies, but ultimately standardized only one medium tank before World War II, and no heavy tank before 1945. The seventh chapter explains Italy's and Japan's shared trend, under mostly Western influence, to light vehicles, despite starting with medium to heavy requirements. The eighth chapter tells of Soviet and German collusion, their innovations, reverse-engineering, and thefts, their rise from practically no tanks to the world's leading users, how the USSR developed the best light, light-medium, medium, and heavy tank series of the interbellum, how Germany developed the longest-produced platform of World War II, and how Czechoslovakia developed fine light tanks that ultimately benefited Germany most. The ninth (final) chapter concludes with explanations and lessons from the whole period, from 1850 to 1939, from Europe to Asia to the Americas, from the Victorian age to World War II.

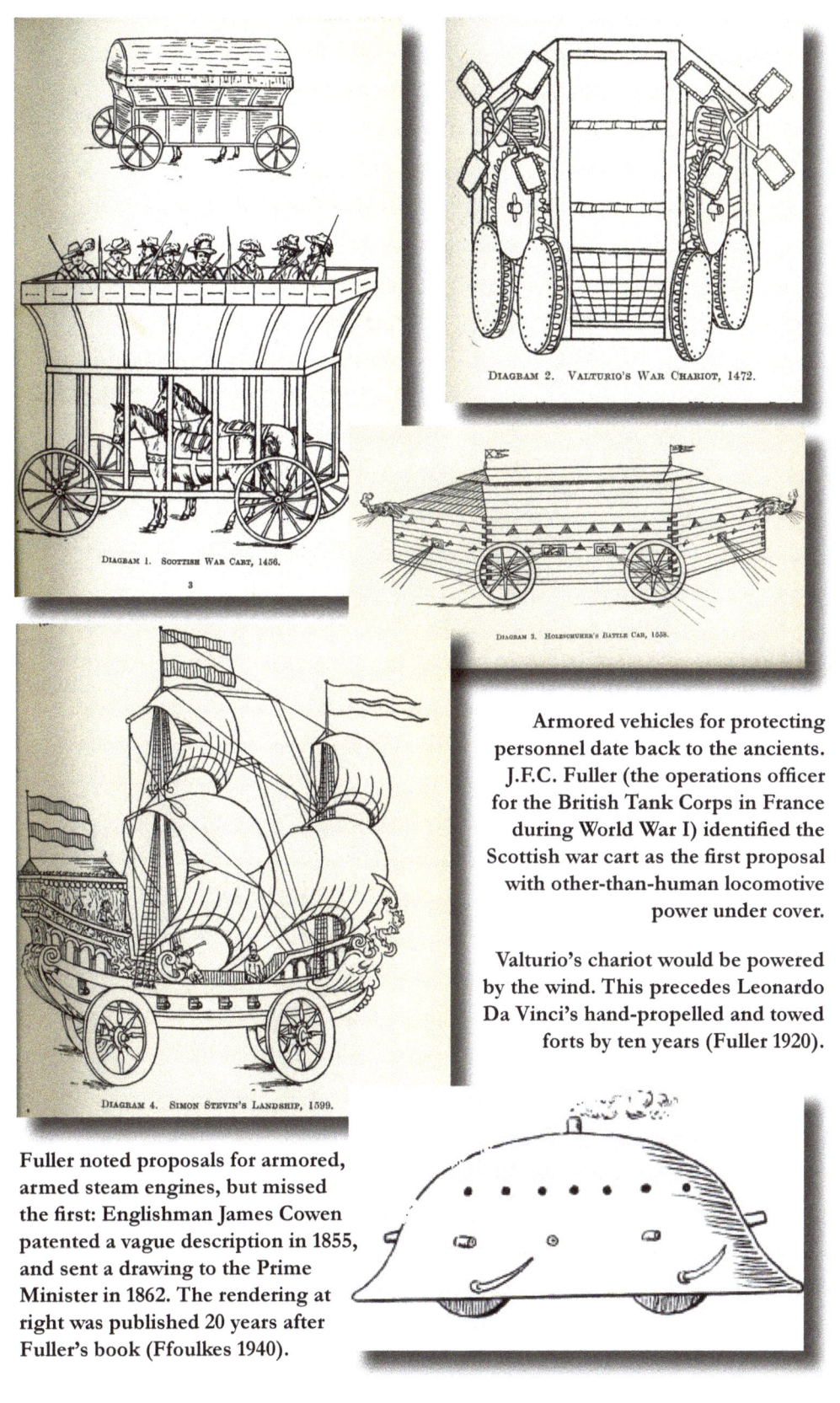

Armored vehicles for protecting personnel date back to the ancients. J.F.C. Fuller (the operations officer for the British Tank Corps in France during World War I) identified the Scottish war cart as the first proposal with other-than-human locomotive power under cover.

Valturio's chariot would be powered by the wind. This precedes Leonardo Da Vinci's hand-propelled and towed forts by ten years (Fuller 1920).

Fuller noted proposals for armored, armed steam engines, but missed the first: Englishman James Cowen patented a vague description in 1855, and sent a drawing to the Prime Minister in 1862. The rendering at right was published 20 years after Fuller's book (Ffoulkes 1940).

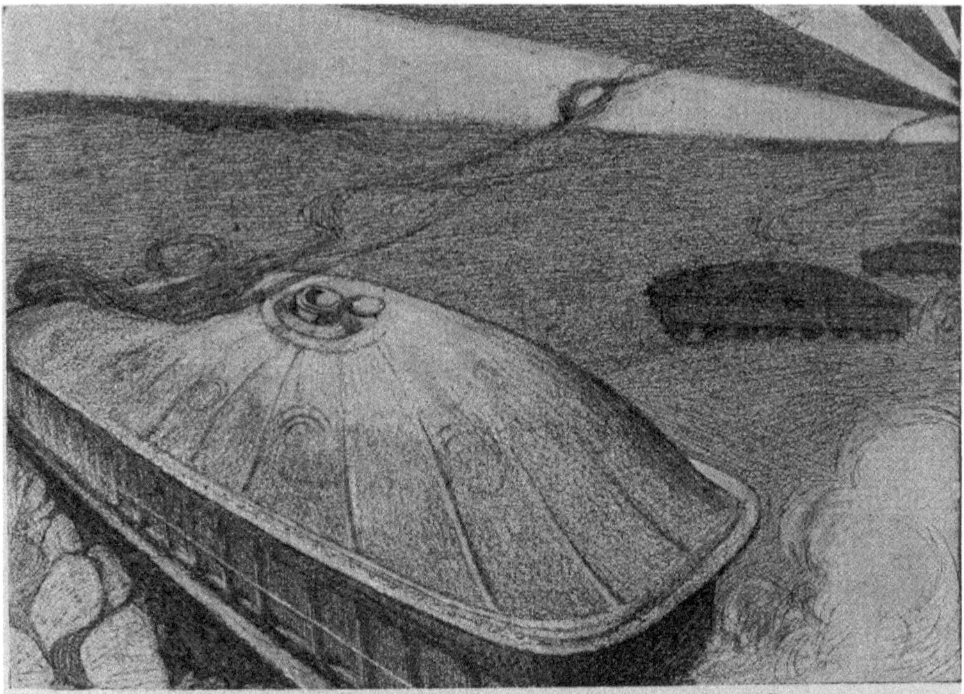

"IT HAD THE EFFECT OF A LARGE AND CLUMSY BLACK INSECT."

This hasty sketch (above) anchored popular cultural expectations for armored fighting vehicles (AFVs), from publication in December 1903 until 22nd November 1916, when newspapers printed images of the iconic British Heavy Mark I tank (below). The sketch was the first illustration of the "Land Ironclads," a short story by H.G. Wells, published by a literary magazine in London. Fourteen "Land Ironclads" are attacking at night (aided by their own searchlights), which helps to explain the artist's shadowy style. They are described via fictional characters, whose first observation goes like this: "It might have been from 80 to 100 feet long – it was about 250 yards away – its vertical side was 10 feet high or so, smooth for that height, and then with a complex patterning under the eaves of its flattish turtle cover. This patterning was a close interlacing of portholes, rifle barrels, and telescope tubes – sham and real – indistinguishable one from the other." Two journalists describe it as "like a fort...Something between a big blockhouse and a giant's dish-cover." It rolled on 16 Pedrail "footed" wheels, driven by steam engines. Semi-automatic rifles were operated remotely from behind armor via electrical controls and cameras.

FIRST PICTURES OF THE TANKS IN ACTION

The Daily Mirror

CERTIFIED CIRCULATION LARGER THAN THAT OF ANY OTHER DAILY PICTURE PAPER

No. 4,092. WEDNESDAY, NOVEMBER 22, 1916 One Halfpenny.

"HUSH, HUSH"—A TANK GOES "GALUMPHANT" INTO ACTION ON THE WESTERN FRONT.

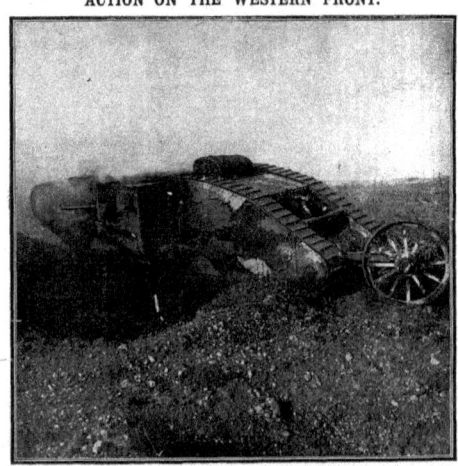

CHAPTER 1

Why Britain was first with tanks

The tank was designed, developed, tried, and deployed during the First World War. The technologies existed before that war, but were first combined during it: armor to protect against kinetic attack (mostly hard and tough species of steel); firearms to attack the enemy; internal combustion engines for producing power; mechanical and electrical transmissions of power; and tracks for imparting motion to the ground.

The class known as "tank" was differentiated by tracks and, eventually, fully revolving turrets. Tracks were the only technologies that needed development. Wheeled automobiles had been armed and armored since 1899. Most proposals for AFVs specified wheels. Imperial Russia's development ended with enormous wheels. Germany was satisfied with armored cars, until Britain introduced tanks.

Britain was first to require (1914) and deploy (1916) tanks. This chapter explains this most important case, before the second chapter looks at the followers.

British foundations

At the time, one would expect Britain to lead. Industrially and financially, the UK came second to the US, but the US was neutral until 1917. Counting the Empire, the UK boasted the largest economy. Britons were still confident in mechanization, industrialization, and invention. Their engineering professions were mature and meritorious. Engineers found rewarding careers in the Royal Artillery (RA) and Royal Engineers (RE). The Army required machines to serve the expanding empire and economize on British soldiers. The increasing rate of imperial wars and the rising threats from Russia and Germany added to the drivers.

The Boer Wars exemplified the Army's capacity for mechanical innovation (more than for tactical innovation). Just in time for the First (1880-1881), the RA acquired large steam-powered wheeled tractors by John Fowler & Company of Leeds (see Table 1). During the Second (1899-1902), it procured about 40 Fowler B5 tractors. In 1900, local RA units asked RE units to armor four of these, which thus became the first steel-armored vehicles deployed during wartime. An armored body, weighing 4.5 long tons (4.6 metric; 5.0 US), was fitted around the boiler, smokebox, firebox, and cab. Each tractor was used to tow an "armoured road train": four artillery guns or armored wagons, each filled with ammunition or 30 men. The experience was not as formative as it should have been for the infantry and cavalry. Road trains were alternatives to railway trains, which later gained the armor from two tractors. The road trains were confined to the best roads, while the army utilized animals elsewhere (Ellis and Chamberlain 1972: 6).

After the Great War, the Army was criticized for ignoring pre-war proposals (see Table 2). In fact, all the proposed armored fighting vehicles (AFVs) were wheeled. The only tracked proposal was for an armored carrier. This proposal arrived in 1912 from an Australian civil engineer (Lancelot E. De Mole). The war would prove he was on the right lines: he drew the running gear with a rhomboidal profile, similar to the first British heavy tanks. Yet his proposal was conceptual. At least

An "armoured road train," with a B5 tractor, three wagons, and a 15-pounder field gun.

one capability was untried (steering by warping the tracks) (Ellis and Chamberlain 1972: 8-10; Harris 1995: 9). The Army was not expected to develop revolutionary vehicles for itself: it could expect Britain's vibrant automotive industry to prove them first. Further, the Army did not expect to be fighting in the most waterlogged corner of Western Europe. Its peacetime requirements were imperial. The French, Austro-Hungarian, and German armies expected to fight in waterlogged corners of the continent, but also turned down proposals for tracked AFVs.

Most wheeled proposals are best characterized as science fiction. In the 1890s, an American writer (Lu Senarens) imagined his hero driving a steam-driven armored truck (the "Magnet"), with an armored gun turret, inspired by naval ironclads. A retired Polish-born, German-educated industrialist (Jan Gotlib Bloch, 1836-1902) wrote a popular and influential forecast (*La Guerre Future*, Paris, 1898), in which firearms would prevent enemy maneuvers, driving the belligerents to mobilize more soldiers and longer defensive lines until they exhaust resources and collapse into revolution. In 1903, the British novelist H.G. Wells envisioned a static war persisting for months, until resolved within hours by "land ironclads," each 80-100 feet (24.4-30.5 m) long, running on 16 driven Pedrail wheels, "each about ten feet [3 m] in diameter," attacking at night with electric lights.

In late 1915, Wells was asked by an engineer at the Ministry of Munitions whether he thought that his Land Ironclad could become practical. A witness paraphrased his reply as: "[it] made good matter for a short story and that was all" (Philip Johnson, "Memo of the Events of 1915-1916," RACTM E2006.1746). After the war, however, Wells blamed the conservatism of military professionals:

> The use of the tank against trenches was an altogether obvious expedient. Leonardo da Vinci invented an early tank, but what military "expert" has ever had the wits to study Leonardo? Soon after the South African War in 1903 there were stories in magazines describing imaginary battles in which tanks figured, and a complete working model of a tank made by Mr. J.A. Corry of Leeds, was shown to the British military authorities – who of course rejected it – in 1911. (Wells 1922: 1,044)

Science fiction did influence wartime designs for large wheeled vehicles, but not the eventual tank. Archibald Low, a British mechanical engineer, later concluded: "Authors who described landships, land ironclads, or whatever they may have called them, no more invented the tank than Jules Verne invented the submarine" (Low 1941: 15). The technologies existed "some years before the opening of the Great War. It only remained for someone to put them together" (1941: 13).

Two types of attachment, for reducing the ground pressure of wheels, were available to the British Army in the decade before World War I, according to official study (Micklethwait 1944).

From 1846, James Boydell patented "footed" wheels, branded as "endless railway." Each wheel carried a "girdle" of plates, of which one or two were successively laid on the ground.

(Top) This drawing shows an "endless railway" on a carriage for launching life boats across soft beaches, supplied by Tipping Limited.

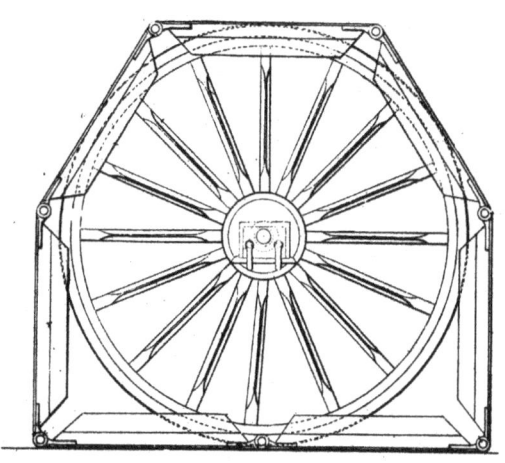

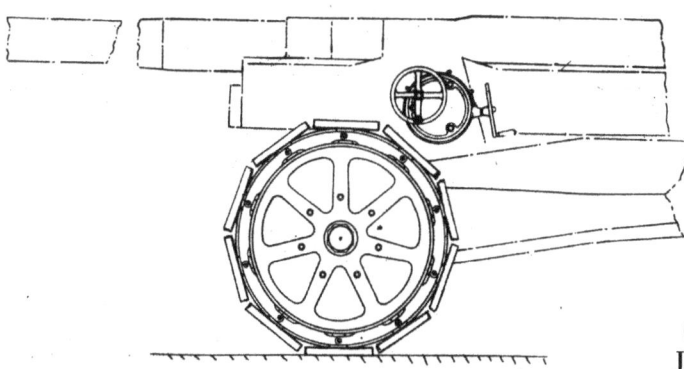

(Middle) This "girdle" of plates was used on British medium and heavy artillery carriages during World War I.

(Bottom) In 1900, Bramah Joseph Diplock (1857-1918) (standing) patented the "Pedrail" wheel, which carried 14 or 16 articulated "feet" (plates), projecting radially so that three always lay flat on the ground, each with a footprint of 95 square inches (61,290 square mm). In 1905, the Army tried a Foster steam tractor with Pedrail wheels (see Table 1). In 1911, Diplock introduced a "chaintrack" with almost square feet. In 1914, he finalized a track with unarticulated feet, wide enough for a single track to support a 1-ton wagon.

American and British tractors

While Britain led the world in steam-powered wheeled tractors, America led in tracked tractors, albeit with some transfer of British technology.

In 1888, Frank Batter of California patented a steam-powered tractor running on an "endless belt" of metal "links," connected by "pins," and capped with wooden "shoes." The vehicle was steered by turning "rollers" in front of respective tracks. JFC Fuller (operations officer for the wartime British tank force in France) estimated that a tank like the British Medium "A" of 1918 could have been executed in 1888 if the authorities had made good use of Batter's patent (Fuller 1920: 10-11, 303).

By 1900, British engineers were experimenting with tracks and oil engines. The most successful was David Roberts, of Richard Hornsby & Sons (Ruston & Hornsby from 1918). In 1905 and 1906, he demonstrated his Number 1 Tracked Tractor to the War Office. It asked him to convert his more powerful wheeled tractor of 1903 to tracks, which became the Number 2. In 1907, this was tried alongside a Steam Log Hauler from Alvin O. Lombard of Maine, which ran on tracks at the rear, skids at the front. Both appeared in the Royal Review in May 1908, when Major Donoghue, of the Mechanical Transport Committee, added a dummy gun to Hornsby's trailer. He suggested armor, without result (Micklethwait 1944: 1.3; Glanfield 2001: 8-10).

In July 1908, the WO announced a competition for "light tractors" (up to 8 tons). Hornsby used the same 70-hp engine and improved running gear on a smaller chassis (Number 3). In 1910, the Army Service Corps (a supply and transport branch) received three variants with 50-hp oil engines, which were quicker to start. In 1911, the WO instigated conversion of the Number 3 to petrol, which offered quicker starts and more power. However, during trials the new Director of Artillery (Major-General Stanley von Donop) revived old questions about requirement.

At the same time, Donop refused a request to try a tracked tractor by Benjamin Leroy Holt (1849-1920) of Stockton, California. Holt had produced steam-powered wheeled tractors since 1890. In 1903, he traveled to England to license Hornsby's

The Hornsby Number 3 is driven by soldiers during the War Office's trials of 1909.

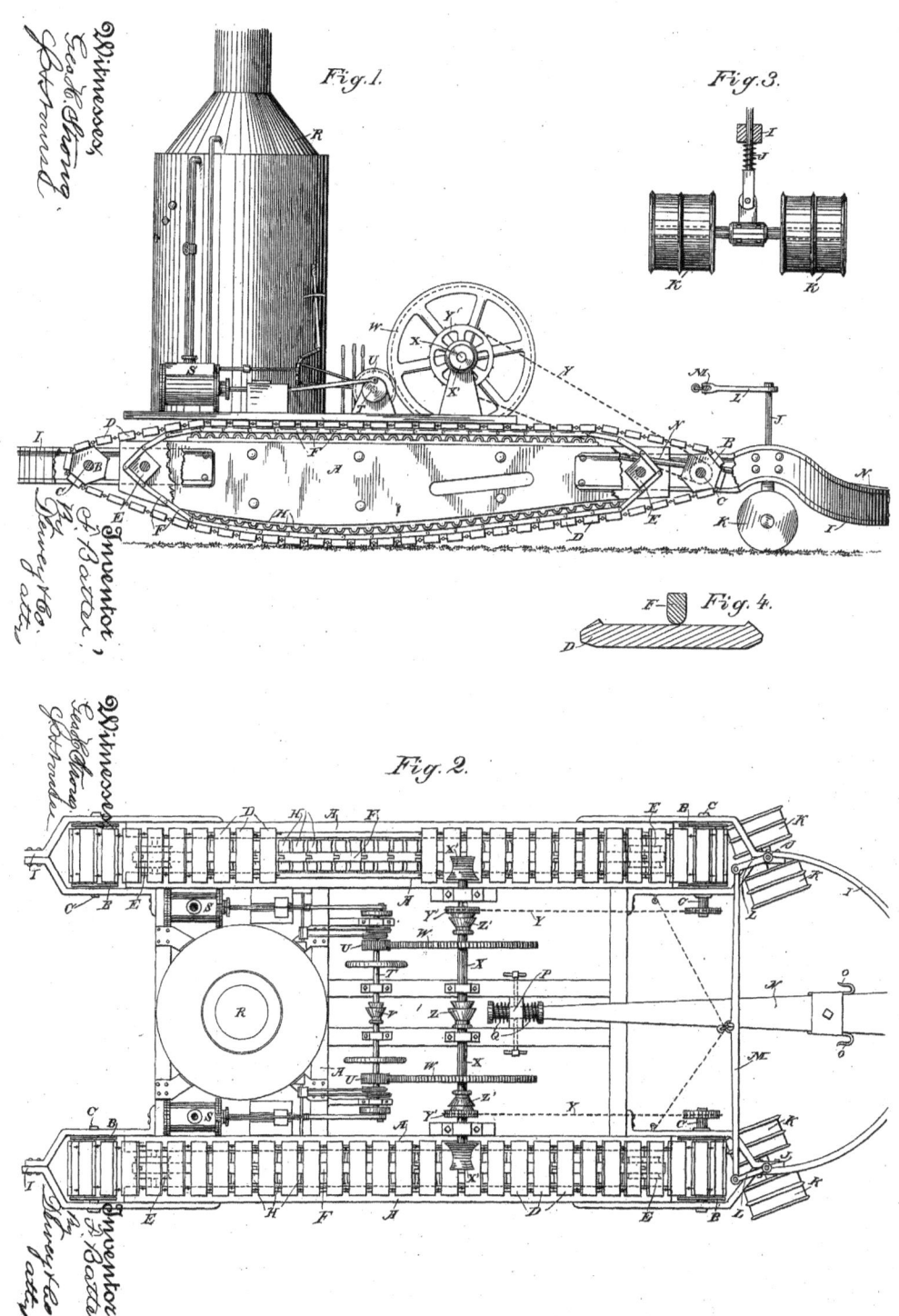

Frank Batter's tracked tractor, according to the two drawings filed with his petition for a patent in February 1888 (source: https://patents.google.com/patent/US382857).

tracks. He eschewed Hornsby's full track steering in favor of a single steered wheel at the front. In 1904, he developed a steam-powered tracked tractor. This he sold in 1906. In 1908, he sold a version with a petrol engine (Holt 45) for work on the Los Angeles aqueduct, prompting orders there and elsewhere for 320 Holt 45s (see Table 1). Their attraction was easier starting and lighter weight.

Holt was one of many American suppliers. In 1910, they produced 4,500 tracked tractors; in 1912, they produced 11,400 (Low 1942: 13). Most were steam engines, taller and heavier than internal combustion competitors, burdensome to ignite, but superior in torque and power. Holt still needed more power, which he achieved with the Holt 60 of 1911. This was the type that broke into the military market. Holt helped himself with aggressive mergers, acquisitions, and marketing. In 1911, he trademarked his tractors as "caterpillars" (the soldiers' nickname for Hornsby tracked tractors), while most talked of "crawlers." In 1912, Holt bought Hornsby's steering patents, which allowed him to introduce a "Baby" Holt 45, without any steered wheel, in 1914 (Orlemann and Haddock 2001).

Army gun tractors

From 1911 to 1914, the US, German, and Austro-Hungarian armies ordered sixty-three Holt 60s for pulling heavy artillery. The US Army moved late, so ended up purchasing more Baby Holt 45s, all for the Field Artillery. (The Motor Transport Corps used only trucks and trailers.)

The British did not deploy mobile heavy artillery, so their only tracked vehicles in service remained the four oil-engine Hornsby tractors held by the RASC since 1910. In 1913, Foster & Company of Lincoln offered its first tracked tractor (actually wheeled at the front, tracked at the rear). The Foster "Centipede" was equivalent to

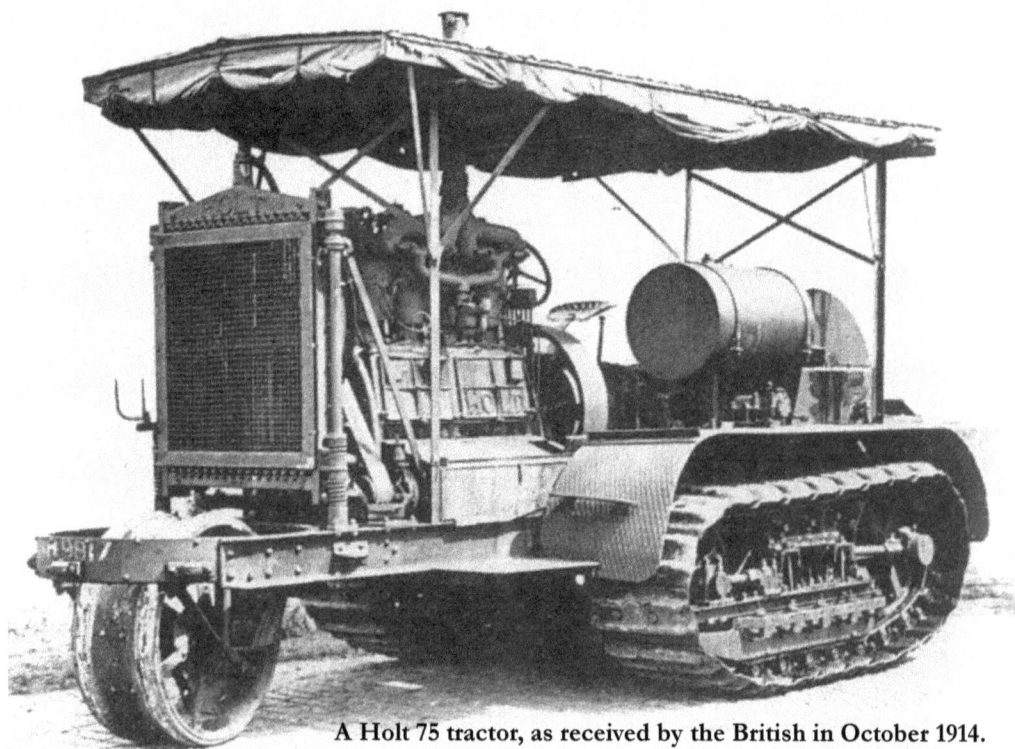

A Holt 75 tractor, as received by the British in October 1914.

the Holt 60 (see Table 1), but no military expressed interest.

In July 1914, a South African mining engineer (Hugh F. Marriott) watched a demonstration of a Holt 60 in Antwerp. By letter, he suggested its potential as an artillery tractor to Colonel Ernest Dunlop Swinton (1868-1951) – Assistant Secretary of the Cabinet's Committee of Imperial Defence (CID). They had met during the Boer Wars when Swinton was official correspondent and historian. Swinton copied the Directorate of Artillery and Directorate of Transport, without result.

In August, a Scottish-American mechanical engineer (Robert Macfie) returned to Britain, fresh from commercial appraisal in Canada of agricultural tractors by Holt and other suppliers. Before that, he had seen Holts at work in Caribbean sugar plantations. He put the idea of military use to unknown officials at the War Office, as suggested by fellow aviators then serving the Royal Flying Corps. However, commercial contacts directed him to the Royal Naval Air Service, which he joined by November.

Colonel Henry Capel Lofft Holden (1856-1937) inherited these proposals. He was an artillery officer, expert in testing guns and explosives, a designer of motor-cycles, and a board member of the Royal Automobile Club and similar organizations. Having retired in 1912, he was recalled in August 1914, as Assistant Director of Mechanical Transport (Fletcher 2001: 23; Glanfield 2001: 15-16, 54-56). He did nothing with the proposals directly. In September, bad weather, mud, and fortification of the front encouraged the BEF to require 5-inch sixty-pounder guns, 6-inch howitzers, and 9.2-inch howitzers. Holden asked Holt's agents to demonstrate suitable tractors. Months earlier, the Holt 75 became available. Thus, the first Holt to reach Britain was a Holt 75, in late October.

Admiralty gun tractors

Meanwhile, retired Rear-Admiral Reginald H.S. Bacon, general manager of Coventry Ordnance Works (in Glasgow, despite the name), proposed to develop 15-inch (381-mm) howitzers that could be transported in two parts, to counter the German 420-mm (16.5-inch) howitzers that had just levelled the fortresses of Liege. After being turned down by the War Office, he approached Winston Churchill (1874-1965) – First Lord of the Admiralty since 1911.

In mid-August, Churchill had supported urgent procurement of armored cars by the Royal Naval Air Service (RNAS) to protect naval air stations in Belgium. The RNAS base in London then became the Admiralty's mechanical research and development center. Bacon persuaded Churchill to order twelve howitzers for the Royal Marines, for protection of naval bases. The first would take until December to reach trials (Churchill 1923: 71-72; Bacon 1940: 196-197). On the same schedule, Bacon procured 97 tractors of the latest British design, by Daimler of Coventy, assembled by Foster & Company of Lincoln (see Table 1). Like the Holts, the Foster-Daimler mounted a spark-ignition engine, but with more power (105 bhp) – enough for the first tanks, as we shall see. It was wheeled, for slightly more speed and range, yet heavier, with more sinkage (Rigby 1919; Ellis and Bishop 1971; Pullen 2007).

Admiralty's Bridge-layer

Each 15-inch howitzer and associated equipment and ammunition would need eight tractors, either by Daimler-Foster or Holt. Bacon showed pictures of Holt tractors in October. Churchill asked whether they could carry troops and weapons across trenches. Bacon thought not (indeed, they were rated for gaps of just 2 feet

Three Foster-Daimler tractors pull a 15-inch barrel, in 1915.

or 0.6 m), so he designed a pushable bridge on a carriage. In November, Churchill authorized a prototype. However, neither man moved with urgency.

Bacon's memoir does not admit this interaction, but skips to 10th December, when the RNAS tried the first Foster-Daimler tractor, including a crossing of a trench, via a timber bridge laid by hand. Bacon urged a mechanical bridge-layer on Foster's general manager, but William Tritton (1875-1946) held no requirement. Bacon took a more developed proposal to Churchill:

> I proposed building a steel bridge longer than the width of a trench and carrying this in front of the tractor, which vehicle would be armored and carry two machine-guns. On arriving at a trench it would drop the bridge over the trench and then itself pass over. When over, it would pick the bridge behind itself. Then it would turn [a]round and go stern first up to the next trench, and repeat the operation. Of course the tractors moved, and steered, equally well whether going forwards or backwards. In addition I proposed to fit two electric head-lights, and two [side] lights, one on each side of the tractor. These would have had glass fronts of about two feet in diameter on which would be outlined the faces of Chinese warriors of that ferocious aspect which Chinese drawings alone can depict. The tractors were noisy machines. So I hoped that the thunder of 40 or 50 of these approaching a trench, and then suddenly switching on their head-lights, might have had a racking effect on the nerves of the men in the trenches. The tractor would then stop on its bridge, switch on the side lights, and enfilade the trench in both directions. (Bacon 1940: 200).

Churchill sent Bacon to the Secretary of State for War (Lord Kitchener), who was too busy dealing with the shortage of artillery shells. Later that month, Churchill ordered Foster to proceed, which ended in June with one unarmored and unarmed bridge-pusher (see Table 2). Nevertheless, Churchill's memoirs misrepresent it as the first "tank" (Churchill 1923: 73; Glanfield 2001: 32-33).

The useful results of the Bridge-Layer were to carry forward Foster's staff and Daimler's engine and gearbox, through various projects to the eventual tank. Tritton was the highest commercial partner in most British tanks of the war. His chief draughtsman William Rigby self-identified as "chief designer, well, draughtsman I suppose you call me…I used to work six in the morning until five at night, but if we were busy we would work all Friday night and not stop until twelve on Saturday afternoon. They were good old days." (Pullen 2007: 153)

In 1916, the British Army acquired 8-inch howtzers and Baby Holt 45s, which did not influence British tanks, but were bases for French tank development from 1915 to 1917.

Armored Holts

Swinton was best qualified to realize the technological and historical trends. He had been commissioned as a Royal Engineer in 1888, but doubled as historian and correspondent. He came to the CID's attention as lead author of a compendium of lessons from the Boer Wars (*The Defence of Duffer's Drift*). In 1910, the CID recruited him to study the Russo-Japanese War. One of his products was a prescription for more machine-guns and better force employment to counter enemy machine-guns (*Handbook on Machine-Gun Tactics*, 1911). In September 1914, the CID appointed him sole official correspondent to the General Headquarters (GHQ) of the British Expeditionary Force (BEF) in France. On 19th October, he read of the upcoming demonstration of the Holt tractor, recalled Marriott, and realized a requirement for armored carriers for machine-gun teams (see Table 2) (Swinton 1932: 79).

On 20th October, he brought the idea to the CID's Secretary (retired Lieutenant-Colonel Maurice Hankey). The next day, he brought retired Captain Thomas G. Tulloch. They had known each other as cadets at the Royal Military Academy Woolwich, before Tulloch joined the artillery. Since 1904, he had managed the Chilworth Gunpowder Company near Guildford. From the start, he passed to the CID what he heard from its German owners. The most important intelligence was German production of an unlicensed derivative of the British Maxim machine-gun for general issue to the infantry (not just specialized fire support units). This was in November 1911, one year before the British Army introduced its own derivative

Supplier	Supplier's state	Name of type	Year of first delivery	Type of engine	Engine power (bhp)	Running gear	Weight	Speed	Range	User states
Burrell-Boydell	Britain	Traction Engine	1857	Steam	15	Wheels, four (Boydell "feet")	9 long, 9.1 metric, 10.1 US			Britain
William Bray	Britain	Traction Engine	1858	Steam	15	Wheels, four	7 long, 7.1 metric, 7.8 US	2.5 mph (4 kph)		Britain
Fowler	Britain	Road Locomotive	1870	Steam	20	Wheels, four (6.5 feet, 2.0 m)	40 long, 40.6 metric, 44.8 US			Germany
Aveling & Porter	Britain	Steam Sapper	1871	Steam	39	Wheels, four (5 feet, 1.5 m)	4.75 long, 4.8 metric, 5.3 US			Britain, France, Turkey, Russia
Fowler	Britain	Artillery Siege Train	1880	Steam	52	Wheels, four (6.5 feet, 2.0 m)	12 long, 12.2 metric, 13.4 US	>8 mph (13 kph)		Britain
Frank Batter	California	Traction Engine	1888 (patent only)	Steam		Tracks, two; Rollers, two				-
M. Scotte	France	Camion à vapeur	1898	Steam	27	Wheels, four	5.9 long, 6.0 metric, 6.6 US	7.5 mph (12 kph)	31 miles (50 km)	France
Fowler	Britain	B5	1899	Steam	65	Wheels, four (7 feet; 2.1 m)	17.5 long, 17.8 metric, 19.6 US	8 mph (13 kph)	17 miles (27 km)	Britain
McLaren	Britain	Colonial	1899	Steam	70	Wheels, four	15 long, 15.2 metric, 16.8 US		12 miles (19 km)	Britain
Keller	Germany	Tractor	1900	Oil	20	Wheels, four (7.5 feet; 2.3 m)	4.9 long, 5.0 metric, 5.5 US	4.9 mph (7.8 kph)		Germany
Charles Renard	France	Road Train	1904	Petrol	50	Wheels, four	3.1 long, 3.1 metric, 3.5 US	45 mph (72 kph)		France
Foster-Diplock	Britain	Number 3 Pedrail	1905	Steam	50	Wheels, four (Pedrail "feet")				Britain
Hornsby	Britain	Number 1 Tracked	1906	Paraffin	20	Tracks, two	16 long, 16.3 metric, 17.9 US			Britain
Austro-Daimler	Austro-Hungary	M06	1907	Petrol	40	Wheels, four	6.9 long, 7 metric, 7.7 US			Austro-Hungary, Germany
Hornsby	Britain	Number 2 Tracked	1907	Oil	70	Tracks, two	8.5 long, 8.6 metric, 9.5 US	7.5 mph (12 kph)	100 miles (161 km)	Britain
Lombard	Maine	Steam Log Hauler	1907	Steam	100	Tracks, two; Skids, two	16.1 long, 16.3 metric, 18 US	4.5 mph (7.2 kph)	10 miles (16 km)	Britain
Daimler-Renard	Britain	Road Train	1908	Petrol	75	Wheels, four	4 long, 4.1 metric, 4.5 US	45 mph (72 kph)		Britain, Germany
Holt	California	Holt 45	1908	Petrol	45	Tracks, two; Wheel, one				-
Austro-Daimler	Austro-Hungary	M08	1908	Petrol	80	Wheels, four	6.9 long, 7 metric, 7.7 US	7 mph (11.5 kph)		Austro-Hungary, Germany
Broom & Wade	Britain	Military Tractor	1909	Paraffin	25	Wheels, four (5'6"; 1.7 m)	6 long, 6.1 metric, 6.7 US	7 mph (11.5 kph)	100 miles (161 km)	-
Stewart	Britain	Tractor	1909	Steam	45	Wheels, four	7 long, 7.1 metric, 7.8 US	8 mph (13 kph)	100 miles (161 km)	-
Thorneycroft	Britain	Tractor	1909	Oil	50	Wheels, four (5'8"; 1.7 m)	7 long, 7.1 metric, 7.8 US	7 mph (11.2 kph)	100 miles (161 km)	Britain

Supplier	Supplier's state	Name of type	Year of first delivery	Type of engine	Engine power (bhp)	Running gear	Weight	Speed	Range	User states
Hornsby	Britain	Number 3 Tracked	1909	Oil	70 (105 in 1911)	Tracks, two	8 long, 8.1 metric, 9.0 US	7.5 mph (12 kph) (doubled in 1911)	100 miles (161 km)	Britain
Hornsby	Britain	Army Service Corps tractor	1910	Oil	50	Tracks, two	8 long, 8.1 metric, 9.0 US			Britain
Austro-Daimler	Austro-Hungary	M09	1911	Petrol	80	Wheels, four	7.2 long, 7.3 metric, 8.0 US	7 mph (11.5 kph)		Austro-Hungary, Germany
Holt	California	Holt 60	1911	Petrol	61	Tracks, two; Wheel, one	8.9 long, 9.1 metric, 10.0 US	3 mph (4.8 kph)		USA, France, Austro-Hungary, Germany
Chatillon-Panhard	France	Tractor	1912	Petrol	40	Wheels, four	2.5 long, 2.5 metric, 2.8 US	11 mph (17 kph)	62 miles (100 km)	France
Austro-Daimler	Austro-Hungary	M12	1912	Petrol	100	Wheels, four (4'11"; 1.5 m)	7.9 long, 8 metric, 8.8 US	7 mph (11.5 kph)		Austro-Hungary, Germany
Lefebvre	France	Tractor	1913	Petrol	40	Wheels, four; pivoted tracks, two	2.2 long, 2.2 metric, 2.4 US			France
Foster	Britain	Centipede	1913	Petrol	60	Tracks, two; Wheels, two	9 long, 9.1 metric, 10.1 US			-
Holt	California	Baby or Muley Holt 45	1914	Petrol	45	Tracks, two	9.2 long, 9.3 metric, 10.25 US			USA, Britain, France
Holt	California	Holt 75	1914	Petrol	83	Tracks, two; Wheel, one	10.4 long, 10.4 metric; 11.5 US	4 mph (6.4 kph)		USA, Britain, France
Foster-Daimler	Britain	Agrimotor	1914	Petrol	105	Wheels, four (8 feet; 2.4 m)	14 long, 14.2 metric; 15.7 US	3.75 mph (6.0 kph)	100 mph (161 km)	Britain
Jeffery (Nash from 1916)	Wisconsin	Quad	1914	Petrol	28	Wheels, four	2.4 long, 2.4 metric, 2.7 US	20 mph (32 kph)		USA, France, Britain
Holt	California	Holt 120	1915	Petrol	120	Tracks, two; Wheel, one	11.8 long, 12.0 metric, 13.25 US	4 mph (6.4 kph)		USA, France, Britain
Killen-Strait	Wisconsin	Tractor	1915	Petrol	30	Tracks, three	2.5 long, 2.6 metric, 2.85 US	4 mph (6.4 kph)		Britain
Bullock	Illinois	Creeping Grip Tractor	1915	Petrol	50	Tracks, two; Wheels, two	8 long, 8.1 metric, 9.0 US			Britain
Bullock	Illinois	California Giant	1915	Petrol	75	Tracks, two; Wheels, two				Britain

Table 1: Tractors tried or acquired by Western militaries, 1857-1915 (as selected by Ellis and Bishop 1971). Notes: dates and states are for military users only; bhp is calculated from nhp with a multiple of 6.5.

(the Vickers). Tulloch proposed to Albert Vickers (a minority shareholder in Chilworth) that Vickers Limited should develop a "landship," with two articulated vehicles, each with a locomotive's steam engine, Hornsby tracks, and an armored superstructure. Each articulated pair was supposed to mount 6 twelve-pounder guns, 12 machine-guns, and 100 men (see Table 2) (Glanfield 2001: 19-20).

Swinton took responsibility for contacting the War Office and Army, Hankey for higher politicians, and Tulloch for suppliers. Both Hankey and Swinton would reproach themselves for ineffectiveness in subsequent months. Swinton held his tongue when meeting the Prime Minister (Herbert Asquith, 1852-1928) later on the 21st. Kitchener missed his appointment on the 22nd, and would doubt the vehicle's survivability when Hankey twice raised the idea. Swinton returned to France on the 23rd, where he failed to persuade the BEF's Chief Engineer (George Fowke).

Nevertheless, the latter wrote to the War Office's Director of Fortifications & Works (Major-General Sir George Scott-Moncrieff). Swinton heard of this by 11th November, when he wrote to Hankey. Marriot had told him the War Office had ordered "several" Holts, but neither man knew for what purpose. In fact, the Holt 75 arrived on 26th October. Holden then ordered a Holt 120, for full trials. It did not arrive until late December. Coincidentally, this is when Hankey, with the excuse of work, got around to writing to the Prime Minister (28th December).

Rollers

Hankey regrettably added a roller to the concept, after seeing a steam roller on Horse Guards Parade. His requirement was brief and technically confused:

> Numbers of large heavy rollers, themselves bullet proof, propelled from behind by motor engines, geared very low, the driving wheels fitted with caterpillar driving gear to grip the ground, the driver's seat armored, and with a Maxim gun fitted. The object of this device should be to roll down the barbed wire by sheer weight, to give some cover to men creeping up behind, and to support the advance with machine-gun fire.

Hankey suggested that the infantry should be further protected by smoke and armored shields, and armed with grapnels and incendiary fuels.

Churchill seconded Hankey, in a letter to the prime minister, dated 2nd January, but prospected a vehicle whose "weight...would destroy all wire entanglements." Like Hankey, Churchill was technically scattered: he talked of "small armored shelters" on "steam tractors" with "caterpillar" tracks. Presumably, these shelters would lack roofs, because he expected troops to throw grenades "out of the top." He talked of "sweeping" the trenches with machine-gun fire, but was unclear whether the fire would come "out of the top" or would need apertures in the sides. He did not mention bridge-layers. Probably, he expected engineers to excavate or construct crossings (he wrote that after the "infantry" had rallied in the first line, the vehicles should "move forward to attack the second line of trenches"). He added a prescription for the vehicles to attack at night, given Bacon's idea of bridge-layers with headlights blazing.

Churchill's letter does not mention rollers. Nonetheless, he appropriated the idea, although he applied it to trenches. He was not distracted by the Army's demonstration of its two Holt tractors on 13th January. On 18th January, he told the Air Division to try two "ordinary steam-rollers," attached side-to-side, to see what weight would "crush" trenches "flat." Churchill seemed to imagine trenches above ground, between revetments, as he had seen in the rocky, dry conditions of the Boer Wars. One of the RNAS engineers visited a demonstration of the Holts on 20th January, which he admired as tractors, but, he realized, lacked capacity for armor. He reported that steam rollers were even less practical. Yet this mere Lieutenant remained in charge of trying Churchill's scheme, which Churchill had demanded within 14 days of his letter. The steam-rollers kept breaking their ties. One was tried alone: despite ropes around the driven wheels, it could not mount a revetment 2 feet (0.6 m) tall. Churchill's memoirs conflate its failure with "Hankey's proposal," even though Hankey meant to flatten wire alone (1923: 76, 538).

Army Holt tractors

The War Office knew none of this, as Churchill feared losing control. Meanwhile, the War Office fluffed its current opportunity to develop tracked AFVs.

On 4th January, Swinton visited London, including the Director of Fortifications & Works. Scott-Moncrieff claimed he could do nothing without a requirement from the BEF, but eventually agreed to set up a committee to investigate the armoring of a Holt or similar tracked vehicle. Swinton nominated Tulloch, and brought him the next day. At lunch, they coincided with Scott-Moncrief's Assistant, who was most enthusiastic (Colonel Louis Jackson). Scott-Moncrief learned from Holden (Assistant Director of Mechanical Transport) that two Holts were at Aldershot. The Director of Artillery (DA) agreed with the merits of investigation, so Scott-Moncrief requested authorization from the Master General of the Ordnance (Donop).

Donop had failed to act on Hankey's articulation of Swinton's idea in recent weeks. Perhaps he was "overwhelmed," as Hankey recalled. Perhaps he retained doubts since 1911 about Hornsby tractors. Either way, he waited for sanction from the very top. On the 7th or 8th, the prime minister showed Churchill's letter to Kitchener, who pressed Donop, who established the committee. Donop thus complied with his superiors, without committing to anything material.

His Committee was unhurried. It viewed the Holts on 13th January, before ordering cross-country trials. On 19th January (the day after the RNAS disproved Churchill's trench-crushing rollers), Tulloch submitted a proposal (see Table 2). He wanted to skip the Holt in favor of his "Landship" of 1911, which he respecified in two less well-armed versions: a "land cruiser; and a "land destroyer." Jackson (the recipient) agreed that the Holt could not carry both armor and armament across a battlefield. Jackson suggested that the tractor could pull an armored trailer. Scott-Moncrief agreed. Both treated the Holt as a stop-gap before a revolutionary vehicle. However, Holden doubted either could be developed in time. He criticized Tulloch as unfamiliar with the challenges. In fact, Holden and Tulloch had history: Tulloch had served as an experimental officer under Holden, before retirement, when both were founding members of the Institute of Automobile Engineers.

Holden limited his ambition to a bridge-layer based on current vehicles. The DA and MGO agreed. Since only the DA, Holden, and Jackson attended the Holt 120's cross-country trials, the bridge-layer advocates dominated. Holden even tried to get the tractor converted into a bridge-layer in advance. Tulloch and Swinton were not invited. The trials waited until 17th February, on the waterlogged artillery ranges at Shoeburyness. The Holt 120 towed a tracked trailer with a 4-ton load (to simulate an armored body, two 40-mm cannons, ammunition, and six men) across barbed wire and a trench. It stuck in a second trench, with the trailer still in the first. The tractor redeemed itself by recovering the steam tractor that had winched

Author	Name	Date	Engine	Power (bhp)	Running gear	Weight	Length	Width	Height	Speed	Armament	Armor	Men
James Cowen	Locomotive Battery	April 1855 (patent)	Steam		Wheels, four, plus tiller wheel at front						14-pounder guns and scythes	"hardened steel"	dozens
James Cowen	Shot- and bomb-proof steam engine.	1862 (letter)	Steam		Wheels, four, plus tiller wheel at front					20 mph (32 kph)	Twelve 3.75-pounder guns; rifles; scythes	"hardened steel"	dozens
H.G. Wells	Land Ironclad	1903 (story)	Steam		Wheels (Pedrail), 16 (10 feet, 3.0 m)		100 feet (30 m)		10 feet (3 m)	6 mph (9.7 kph)	Semi-automatic rifles	12 inches (305 mm)	hundreds
"Tom" Tulloch	Landship	November 1911	Steam		Tracks, Hornsby, on two articulated vehicles						Six 12-pounder guns; twelve machine-guns	Bullet-proof	100
Ernest Swinton	(armored Holt)	20th October 1914	Petrol	75	Tracks (Holt)						Machine-guns	Bullet-proof	
Thomas Hetherington	Hetherington Proposal	November 1914	Diesel		Wheels, three (200 feet, 61 m)	800 long, 813 metric, 896 US					One 12-inch gun	30 inches (762 mm)	hundreds
William Tritton and Rigby	Foster's Portable Bridge Machine	December 1914	Petrol	105	Wheels, four (8 feet, 2.4 m)					3.75 mph (6.0 kph)	Two to four machine-guns (none on pilot of June 1915)	none	2
Maurice Hankey	Large heavy roller	28th December 1914	Petrol		Roller at front, Tracks (Holt) at rear						One machine-gun	Bullet-proof	1
Thomas Hetherington	Revised Hetherington Proposal	December 1914 - January 1915	Diesel	800	Wheels, three (40 feet; 12.2 m)	300 long, 305 metric, 336 US	100 feet (30 m)	80 feet (24 m)	46 feet (14 m)	8 mph (12.9 kph)	Six 4-inch guns	3 inches (76 mm)	hundreds
Tom Tulloch	Land Cruiser	January 1915	Steam		Tracks (Hornsby), four, across two articulated vehicles						Four 40-mm cannons; two machine-guns; electrified rail	Two layers of 7 mm each	100
Tom Tulloch	Land Destroyer	January 1915	Steam		Tracks, Hornsby, on two articulated vehicles						two to three machine-guns	Two layers of 7 mm each	100
Louis Jackson	(Holt tractor-trailer)	January 1915	Petrol	120	Tracks (Holt), four	4-ton load on trailer					Two cannons	Bullet-proof	6
Murray Sueter		Early February 1915	Diesel	160 (2x80)	Tracks (Pedrail), two, in line	24 long, 24.4 metric, 26.9 US	32 feet (9.8 m)		>12 feet (3.4 m)		One 12-pounder gun; two 6-pounder guns.	Armor	8
W.E.B. Crompton	Self-Moving Armoured Fort	19th February 1915	Petrol	105	Wheels, four (8 feet, 2.4 m)	24 long, 24.4 metric, 26.9 US	36 feet (11.0 m)	11 feet (3.4 m)			Two machine-guns, on in each front corner turret	0.3 inch (8 mm)	50 (of which: 48 infantry)
W.E.B. Crompton	(above with winch and anchor)	22nd February 1915	Petrol	105	Wheels, four (8 feet, 2.4 m)	23 long, 23.4 metric, 25.8 US	36 feet (11.0 m)	13 feet (4.0 m)			Two machine-guns, on in each front corner turret	0.3 inch (8 mm)	50 (of which: 48 infantry)
W.E.B Crompton	(larger version of above)	22nd February 1915	?	525	Wheels, four (8 feet, 2.4 m)	126 long, 128 metric, 141 US	36 feet (11.0 m)	18 feet (5.5 m)			Two machine-guns, on in each front corner turret	5 inches (127 mm)	50 (of which: 48 infantry)
Landship Committee	Self-Moving Cupola Type A	22nd February 1915	Petrol	105	Wheels, four (15 feet, 4.6 m)	25 long, 25.4 metric, 28.0 US						0.3 inch (8 mm)	50
Landship Committee	Self-Moving Cupola Type B	22nd February 1915			Tracks (Pedrail)	25 long, 25.4 metric, 28.0 US						0.3 inch (8 mm)	50
Bramah Diplock and James Lowe	Self-Moving Cupola Type B	c.25th February 1915	Petrol	46	Tracks (Pedrail), two, across two vehicles fixed in line	25 long, 25.4 metric, 28.0 US	38 feet (11.6 m)	12.5 feet (3.8 m)	10.5 feet (3.2 m)	8-12 mph (12.9-19.3 kph)	One 12-pounder gun in top-mounted turret	0.3 inch (8 mm)	50
W.E.B. Crompton	Revised Self-Moving Cupola Type B	4th March 1915	Petrol	160 (2x80)	Tracks (Pedrail), two, across two vehicles fixed in line	25 long, 25.4 metric, 28.0 US	40 feet (12.2 m)	12.5 feet (3.8 m)	10.5 feet (3.2 m)	4.5 mph (7.2 kph)	none	0.3 inch (8 mm)	70
Tritton and Rigby	Foster Trench Tractor (and trailer)	19th March 1915	Petrol	105	Wheels, four (15 feet, 4.6 m)	36 long, 36.6 metric, 40.3 US	48' (14.6 m); 37' (11.3 m) by May	8.5 feet (2.6 m)	15 feet (4.6 m)		Machine-gun in turret firing rearwards. Artillery gun in lieu of 70 infantrymen	Armor	70

Designer	Name	Date	Engine	Weight	Propulsion	Length	Width	Height	Speed	Armament	Armour	Crew
Robert Macfie	Armoured Caterpillar (I)			50	Tracks, four (later: two tracks and two wheels)							56
R.E.B Crompton	Self-Moving Cupola Type B Mark II	22nd April 1915	Petrol	160 (2x80)	Tracks (Pedrail), two, across two articulated vehicles	25 long, 25.4 metric, 28.0 US	40 feet (12.2 m)	12.5 feet (3.8 m)	9 feet (2.7 m)	4.5 mph (7.2 kph)	Apertures for small arms; grenade-launchers	0.47 inch (12 mm)	30
R.E.B Crompton	Self-Moving Cupola Type B Mark IIa	24th April 1915	Petrol	150 (2x75)	Tracks (Bullock), four, across two articulated vehicles	28 long, 28.4 metric, 31.3 US	44 feet (13.4 m)				Apertures for small arms; grenade-launchers	0.47 inch (12 mm)	10
Ernest Swinton	Machine-Gun Destroyer	7th May 1915	Petrol		Tracks (Hornsby), two (possibly a track at front too)					4 mph (6.4 kph)	One 40-mm cannon, two machine-guns	0.47 inch (12 mm)	2
William Tritton	(armoured) Portable Bridge Machine	1st June 1915	Petrol	105	Wheels, four (8 feet; 2.4 m)						One machine-gun	Bullet-proof	
William Tritton	Armoured wagon or fort	3rd June 1915	Petrol	105	Wheels, four (8 feet; 2.4 m)						Two machine-guns	Bullet-proof	
William Tritton	Armoured wagon or fort (electric)	5th June 1915	Electric		Wheels, four (8 feet; 2.4 m)	14 long, 14.2 metric, 15.7 US 18 long, 18.3 metric, 20.2 US					Two machine-guns	Bullet-proof	
Scott-Moncrieff	(reaction to Mark IIa)	5th June 1915	Petrol	150 (2x75)	Tracks (Bullock), two, across two articulated vehicles	28 long, 28.4 metric, 31.3 US	44 feet (13.4 m)				Two 40-mm cannons towards the front, two machine-guns behind, each in a turret	0.47 inch (12 mm)	30
Department of Trench Warfare	Armoured Land Cruiser	16th June 1915	Petrol	180-206	Tracks (Pedrail), two, across two articulated vehicles	35 long, 35.6 metric, 39.2 US	40 feet (12.2 m)	13 feet (4.0 m)	8.5 feet (2.6 m)	10 mph (16.1 kph)	Flamethrower, 3 machine-guns	plates, chain nets, springs	6
Landships Committee	Caterpillar Machine-Gun Destroyer	June 1915	Petrol		Tracks					4 mph (6.4 kph)	One 40-mm cannon; two machine-guns	0.47 inch (12 mm)	10
General Staff preferences	Caterpillar Machine-Gun Destroyer	2nd July 1915	Petrol							4 mph (6.4 kph)	Six 40-mm cannons, four machine-guns	0.47 inch (12 mm)	25
R.E.B Crompton	Self-Moving Cupola Type B Mark III	2nd July 1915	Petrol	150 (2x75)	Tracks (Bullock), four, across two articulated vehicles	28 long, 28.4 metric, 31.3 US	44 feet (13.4 m)	12.5 feet (3.8 m)	9.5 feet (2.9 m)		Four 40-mm cannons, each in a turret; four machine-guns	0.47 inch (12 mm)	6
R.E.B Crompton	Self-Moving Cupola Type B Mark IIIa	Early July 1915	Petrol	150 (2x75)	Tracks (Bullock), four, across two articulated vehicles	28 long, 28.4 metric, 31.3 US	44 feet (13.4 m)	12.5 feet (3.8 m)	7.5 feet (2.3 m)		Two 40-mm cannons, each in a turret	0.47 inch (12 mm)	6
Robert Macfie	Armoured Caterpillar (II)	Mid-August 1915	Petrol		Tracks, two, wheels, two, at rear						Two machine-guns	Bullet-proof	c.6
R.E.B Crompton	Self-Moving Cupola Type B Mark IV	19th August 1915	Petrol	150 (2x75)	Tracks (Killen-Strait), six, across two articulated vehicles	25 long, 25.4 metric, 28.0 US	44 feet (13.4 m)	12.5 feet (3.8 m)	6 feet (1.8 m)		Two 40-mm cannons, each in a turret	0.47 inch (12 mm)	6
Tritton-Wilson-Rigby	Number 1 Lincoln Machine (Little Willie)	31st August 1915	Petrol	105	Tracks (Bullock), two, two wheels at rear were added during construction	16.5 long, 16.8 metric, 18.5 US	19'3" (5.9 m); 26.5 feet (8.1 m) with wheels	9'5" (2.9 m)	10'2" (3.1); 8'3" (2.5 m) less turret	2 mph (3.2 kph)	One 40-mm gun in turret (not completed); up to six machine-guns firing through apertures in sides	0.4 inch (10 mm)	6
Tritton-Wilson-Rigby	Centipede (Big Willie)	By 28 September 1915	Petrol	105	Tracks (Tritton-Wilson), two	28 long, 28.4 metric, 31.3 US	25'5" (7.75 m); 32.5 feet (9.9 m) to wheels	13'9" (4.2 m)	8'2" (2.5 m)	2 mph (3.2 kph) doubled on 29th)	One 40-mm in side sponson, one 75-mm in other side sponson (replaced by 57-mm guns in December)	0.4 inch (10 mm) delivered with 12 mm at front	8

Table 2: British proposals for tanks, 1855-1915 (sources as per main body text).

it out of the trench. Jackson advocated for a more powerful and longer vehicle, but the MGO moved him to a Directorate for Chemical Warfare. Donop delegated Scott-Moncrief to find a developer, which ended with Holden writing a brief reply, containing the phrase "I cannot," before he named Hornsby as the "only" experienced company (Churchill 1923: 76; Fletcher 2001: 25; Glanville 2001: 25-29).

The eventual tank would prove them unambitious: it was ready within 11 months. They had good reasons to doubt the Holt's performance on a real battlefield, but not further development. Perhaps they were biased by their offices: the DA and MGO (another artilleryman) urgently required tractors for guns. Holden made his own job easier by reserving Holts as transport. Unintentionally, their dismissal of tracked AFVs was advantageous technologically, in that the eventual tank had superior running gear to any of the vehicles developed from Holt tractors.

The British used Holts only as tractors. The War Office ordered another 10 Holt tractors in March, another 65 by June, and a total of 2,093 by the Armistice, including 442 produced under license by Hornsby from 1917 to 1918. Western militaries received more than 5,000 Holts, including 676 Holt 120s, which was most powerful but difficult to steer (Glanfield 2001: 15-16; Orlemann and Haddock 2001).

Big wheel gunships and small wheel wagons

The Admiralty wasted the winter on extreme proposals for hand carts and big-wheeled gunships. The unintended seed was Macfie's campaign to get Holts for the RNAS as gun tractors and AFVs, in place of the armored cars he was servicing as Field Repair Officer. In November, the RNAS Transport Officer (Flight-Commander Thomas G. Hetherington), who had flown with Macfie before the war, facetiously suggested a fighting compartment large enough to take 12-inch guns, with a pair of wheels like the Ferris wheel at Earls Court to cross the Rhine. The commander of

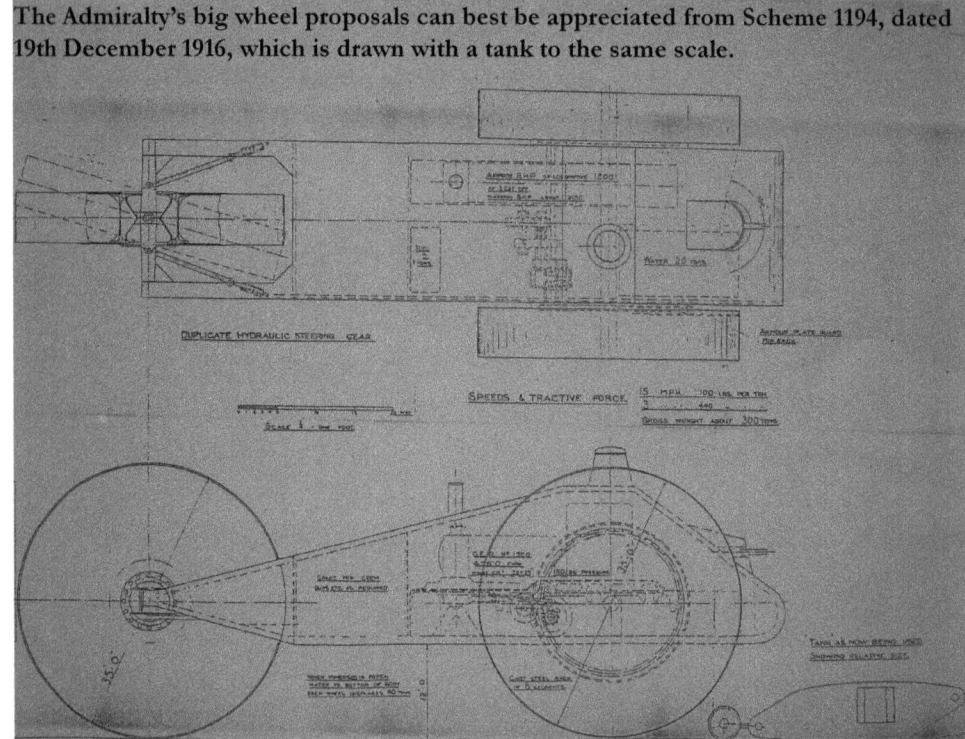

The Admiralty's big wheel proposals can best be appreciated from Scheme 1194, dated 19th December 1916, which is drawn with a tank to the same scale.

A standard pushable Pedrail carriage is demonstrated with a mock shield in june 1915.

the Air Division (Murray Sueter) encouraged further specifications, which added up to an 800-ton vehicle (813 metric; 896 US). Sueter encouraged something smaller.

Sueter also proposed the smallest armored vehicle imaginable: a bullet-proof shield on a pushable carriage with a single wheel. In early December, Churchill authorized 20 such carriages. He included this prospect in his letter to the prime minister on 5th January. Captain Gordon Macready (a Royal Engineer assigned to an experimental establishment at St. Omer) saw the product:

> A naval petty officer had invented an armor-plated shield some five feet high and six wide on small wheels with a shaft behind. The idea was that four or five men should push the shield forward against the enemy, being protected by the armor, thus counteracting the machine-gun which was the cause of our military stagnation. The shield, unfortunately, was only maneuverable on the smoothest ground, and only afforded protection against fire from the immediate front. (Macready 1965: 17)

On 13th January, Sueter received from Pedrail a pushable truck on a single exceptionally wide track, marketed as "Colonial Wagon," for loads of 1 ton. Sueter applied the track to both the pushable shield and Macfie's proposal. A seed for the latter might have been the deployment of the first 15-inch howitzer in January: the Foster-Daimler tractors failed to pull it up the hill out of Boulogne (Bacon 1940: 235). The most powerful tractor with a spark-ignition engine in Britain was the Holt 120, but only the War Office was buying Holts. Sueter proposed that something like a small submarine could be mounted on lengthened Pedrail tracks.

Around the same time, Hetherington finished his "Revised Proposal" (see Table 2). He calculated that wheels must be at least 40 feet (12.2 meters) in diameter to roll over trenches. (He estimated the width of the front wheels at 13 feet 4 inches (4 m). This might explain why, on 18th January, Churchill specified the two rollers with a combined front of 12 to 14 feet.) Hetherington specified two wheels at the front, and a steered wheel at the rear. He reduced weight by armoring the engine compartment and turrets, but leaving the frame exposed and reducing the armament to six 4-inch guns (across three turrets). Still, the vehicle was estimated at 300 long tons (305 metric; 336 US). Churchill's naval staff sensibly assessed that such a large vehicle would be shot to pieces before its guns could counter the shooters.

Nevertheless, Hetherington and two fabulously wealthy RNAS officers who had known Churchill since before the war (the Duke of Westminster and the banker

Albert Gerald Stern) contrived a dinner party with him on 14th February.

Sueter was excluded, but he found out the next day. For 16th February, he arranged a demonstration on Horse Guards Parade of a Pedrail wagon. Churchill asked how a single-track automobile could be steered. Sueter suggested shifting water as ballast, before suggesting two tracks in parallel, so that the inner track could be braked. Finally, he suggested converting armored cars to tracks. Yet Churchill still wanted a vehicle that could span a trench and drop infantrymen inside, while Sueter was offering only fire-support vehicles (Glanfield 2001: 64-66).

Wheeled Trench Enfilader

Churchill decided to shift responsibility to a Landships Committee under the Director of Naval Construction (Eustace Tennyson d'Eyncourt). Churchill named it after Tulloch's proposal, but focused on Hetherington's. Hetherington was one of only two other members. The other was the Royal Naval Division's transport officer (Colonel of Royal Marines Wilfrid Dumble, formerly manager of London General Omnibus Company, before that a RE officer).

They convened first on 20th February, with Tritton and one of Bacon's representatives. The latter two were invited only to hear Churchill cancel the 30 bridge-layers, except for one system to be completed for experiment. The remaining three men were told to consider Hetherington's "Revised Proposal."

On the way out, Hetherington asked Dumble to recommend an expert on traction. Dumble suggested someone he had consulted five days earlier on the bridge-layer: R.E.B. Crompton, an electrical and road engineer. In October, Dumble had consulted Crompton about the collapse of Belgian roads. In December, Dumble invited him to view the Daimler-Foster tractor, when Bacon told both men about his proposal for a bridge-layer.

Crompton subsequently wrote to Dumble with a proposal on how he could help Bacon, but Tritton was in charge by then. They had worked for competing electrical companies, until 1905, when Tritton joined Foster, just in time to see the Foster-Diplock tractor rejected by the WO Military Transport Committee, of which Crompton was a member. Crompton left that Committee in 1905, but was still advising Holden when Tritton offered his semi-tracked "Centipede" in 1913.

By 1915, Crompton was almost 70 years old and out of touch. He had used steam tractors as an army officer in India during the 1860s, and South Africa from 1899-1902, but his true specialty was electrical. With the retired rank of Lieutenant-Colonel, and honorary rank of Colonel (from the electrical engineer volunteers of the Boer Wars), he pushed for recall into government. Only Dumble indulged him.

Dumble returned to Crompton on 15th February, to discuss the bridge-layer. Crompton revived Bacon's/Churchill's proposal for a trench-spanning infantry carrier, except that the trench would be enfiladed by a machine-gun turret at each front corner. Crompton suggested lengthening and widening a Foster-Daimler tractor or equivalent competitor (see Table 2). Crompton invited Holden's superior (the Director of Supplies) to discuss this over lunch on 19th February, but the latter bowed out. Crompton was ready with the same proposal when Dumble and Hetherington sought him out on the afternoon of 20th February (Ellis and Chamberlain 1972: 17; Harris 1995: 19-24; Glanfield 2001: 68-75).

Two days later, the Landships Committee accepted what Crompton proposed. To wit: the Committee accepted a requirement imagined by Bacon, and seconded by Crompton, neither of whom had seen the current front, served in any of the arms, or received any undertakings from the users. The Committee was composed of only three people, whose sum authorities were for ships, airships, armored cars, and trucks – and all for Royal Naval use alone.

The Committee was serving only Churchill directly, whose confidence ran ahead of his judgment. Churchill later claimed he was procuring for the benefit of all ground forces, including the Army, but at the time he hid from the Army. He wanted the RNAS to gain three squadrons of "landships," to support the fledgeling Naval Division in the capture of enemy trenches, on the most coastal corner of the Allied front. This narrow market helps to explain, but does not excuse, the Admiralty's requirement for trench-enfilading personnel carriers, without any user requirement or a practical design.

Crompton's written proposal was entitled "A Self-Moving Armoured Fort for the Attack and Destruction of Enemy's Trenches" (see Table 2). He lowered the weight slightly from his proposal of 19th February, but the Committee raised the weight limit to 25 long tons (25.4 metric; 28 US). This was the capacity of current roads, as standardized by Crompton in 1910, when engineer to the government's Road Board. The Committee approved the project as "Self-Moving Cupola Type A," and specified development of the Foster-Daimler tractor into something three times longer, with wheels almost twice the size, at 15 feet (4.6 m) in diameter. When Crompton visited Foster on the 26th, Tritton disinterestedly suggested that the bridge-layer's three-wheeled platform would suffice. Crompton agreed in the moment, although by the time he got home he realized his mistake. Yet he did not have the nerve to confront Tritton again, so he sent his partner (Lucien Legros, otherwise a designer of generators). Tritton sent Legros away with a letter refuting Crompton's authority and the requirement for a troop-carrier.

On 4th March, Crompton told the Landship's Committee that Tritton's platform would not be able to carry more than 30 infantrymen. The only person Crompton needed to persuade was Hetherington, because Dumble had taken a job with a commercial armaments supplier. Dumble was replaced by an appointee from the Admiralty's Department for Contracts, who was even less qualified to judge. His skill was to account in ways that did not alert the Treasury (and thence the WO).

Tritton's bridge-layer is tested in Foster's yard, Lincoln, by Hetherington (at the horizontal wheel).

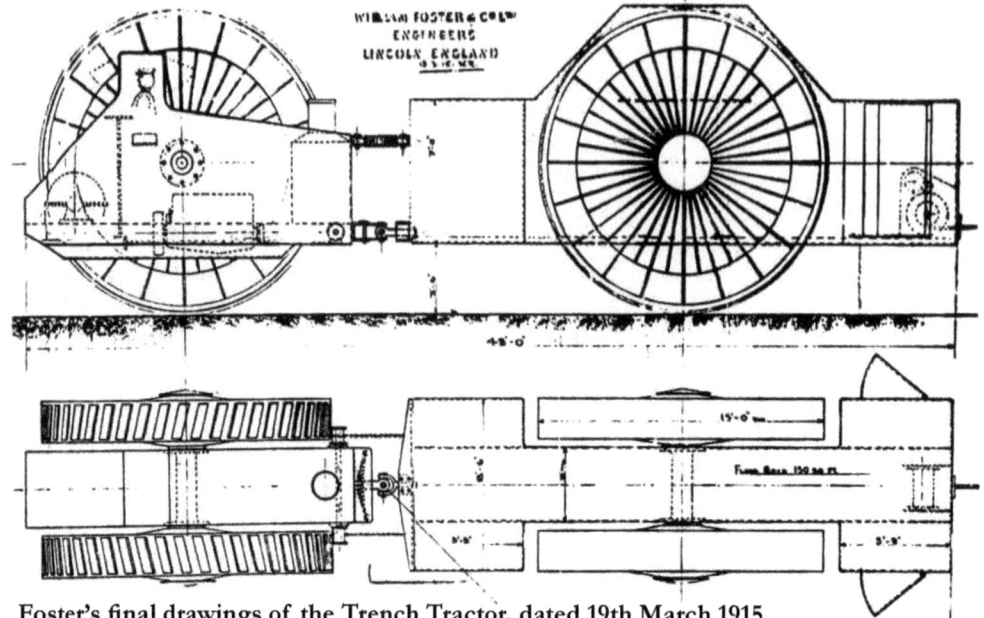

Foster's final drawings of the Trench Tractor, dated 19th March 1915.

Tracked Self-Moving Cupola

Macfie had been present on 22nd January. He pressed for Holt tracks, so Crompton added a tracked version, but with Pedrail tracks, in which he had a conflict of interest. He had tested Diplock's first tractor (1894) and co-founded Diplock's first company (1897). Pedrail tracks suited Churchill too, who, by then, was enamored with the Pedrail wagon, and did not want to alert the WO by expressing interest in Holts (William Rigby to David Fletcher, 18th May 1967, in RACTM Tanks World War 1).

However, Crompton knew Diplock as unreliable, and that the current Pedrail track needed to be made three times longer and correspondingly robust. Nobody had yet tried Pedrail tracks on an automobile. Crompton undertook to investigate alternatives, but two days later reported none, without viewing any from Hornsby, Foster, or Holt – or requesting information from the American suppliers, most of whom were already represented in Britain.

The Committee approved the tracked version as "Self-Moving Cupola Type B," for which Diplock and his chief draughtsman (James Lowe) designed two tracks in line. The two running gears would be articulated, but would carry a single rigid platform. Influenced by Sueter, Diplock and Low drew a submarine-shaped superstructure, and a turret, carrying a 12-pounder gun. They produced the outline drawing on 4th March. Crompton did away with the turret and lengthened the platform slightly in order to increase the load to 70 infantrymen. He replaced the floor hatch from his first proposal with two side doors. The Landships Committee approved on the same day he presented his sketch.

Pedrail Transport Ltd. lacked capacity to assemble, so Crompton approached Foden (best known for lorries), which contracted on 12th March to serve as lead contractor and assembler. Legros arranged a Rolls-Royce engine (already acquired for RNAS armored cars) for each track. Crompton specified driving positions at both ends, so needed a separate contractor to develop a revolutionary transmission linked across two separately powered running gears (Glanfield 2001: 77-79).

The chassis of Crompton's Mark I Self-Moving Cupola would have looked like this, although this particular chassis was finished in June 1916 as the platform for a transport vehicle, long after the cancellation of Crompton's program.

Foster Trench Tractor

In March, D'Eyncourt asked Stern to administer the Committee. Stern later claimed to be already sceptical of Crompton, and preferential to Tritton:

> I saw that you were the only man in sight who could develop the idea of the Landship into a useful weapon of war, because you had a unique experience of heavy traction and the rare combination of highly technical knowledge and the commonsense of a successful businessman. (Stern to Tritton, 19th November 1917, in RACTM Tanks World War 1)

Stern's confidences explain Tritton's assertiveness. On 19th March, he suddenly showed a model of a "Foster Trench Tractor," with 15-foot wheels, and an armored trailer rated for 70 men or an artillery piece. Tritton promised to meet Crompton's specifications, within three months, without the risks of tracks. Tritton later admitted it would have been cramped and under-powered, but blamed the specifications, lack of user involvement, and urgency. D'Eyncourt wanted to order one. The next morning, Churchill called in D'Eyncourt, Hetherington, Crompton, and Legros. By the end of the day, Churchill authorized six Foster Trench Tractors and twelve Crompton-Pedrails. Still, he hid all procurements from the Treasury.

The first Foster Trench Tractor was expected in June, the first Crompton-Pedrail in July. However, Foden suffered a labor dispute, so a new lead contractor was needed. Armor steel had not been secured (so as not to tip off the rest of government). On news that the Germans were perforating the infantry's armor shields with reversed bullets, Crompton increased the armor thickness from 8 mm to 12 mm. To save weight, he lowered the superstructure, which meant passengers would be forced to sit or crouch. Worse, Diplock proved as unreliable as he had before the war. He never finished drawings suitable for production.

Crompton and Hetherington realized a change in requirement after a belated visit to the front on 21st April. Each enemy trench zig-zagged so that only a few yards at a time were exposed to enfilading fire. They prescribed that the vehicle should park alongside each zig or zag, so that passengers could throw grenades. Crompton then specified a grenade-thrower so that the vehicle could remain 100 yards away. Apertures were provided for small-arms fire (see Table 2).

Track research

Also in April, Crompton belatedly researched alternative tracks, although still no British ones (except Pedrail). Holden was one influence: in 1905, he condemned Hornsby tracks for trapping stones in the large hinges between links, and stressing the joints (the action was likened to a nutcracker). From 1906, Hornsby, through a subsidiary (Tractor Transport Limited), offered "light" tracks for cars. Holden's Military Transport Committee viewed them but did not order any. In 1910, Foster placed Hornsby's light tracks on a steam-engined tractor, which it sold to Northern Light, Power & Coal Company of Yukon, Canada. Tritton went on to produce his Centipede tractor in 1913 (see Table 1), with steel tracks, adjustable in camber. He described them as free of nutcracker action, but Holden expected the problem in all tracks. It went to Paraguay without military interest. An order from Java for 50 Centipedes was interrupted by war. Tritton was not asked to develop tracks until September 1915, when he recycled the name "Centipede" (Pullen 2007: 24-25).

Between Centipede tractor (1913) and Centipede tank (1915), only American tracks were tried in Britain. Development of tracked Holts was suggested by Macfie to officials and suppliers in September 1914, but his decision to join the RNAS in October ended whatever influence he had on the WO. Nevertheless, in the same month the WO received a similar suggestion from Swinton. Yet the WO waited for a Holt 120 to arrive (January) before trying Holts experimentally. It then eschewed tracks, except for hauling (February). In March, Tritton said to Legros, "The caterpillar system is no bloody good for the job." This has been interpreted as disinterest in tracks in general (Glanfield 2001: 77, 105), but Tritton was referring to Holt's.

In April, Macfie heard enough to object to Crompton's neglect of Holt tractors and his requirement for trench-enfilading personnel carriers. He persuaded Sueter to authorize conversion of an Alldays & Onion four-wheeled 5-ton lorry chassis to

The Foster Centipede tractor, as marketed in 1913.

four track units of his own design (Table 2). The two track units at the front would be used for steering; the two at the rear would be driven.

On 22nd April, Sueter ordered a small engineering firm (Nesfield & Mackenzie, of London), which was already supplying mountings for anti-aircraft guns, to work to Macfie's orders. However, six weeks later the company asked to be replaced, complaining of Macfie's attitude. Contradictorily, the company offered a design of its own (with two track units, steered by braking). The firm presented a model on 1st July, to Crompton, Hetherington, and others at the RNAS home station, but Macfie claimed it as his. He explained that it was meant only to demonstrate how tracked vehicles climb: its tracks were just bicycle chains, driven by electric motors. Nesfield countered that Macfie's designs were all four-tracked. Indeed, the only surviving drawing of a two-track vehicle by Macfie is dated 19th August; and this was supposed to be steered by trailing wheels, not braking. Macfie drew its running gear as an open frame, tallest and forward-sloped at the front to aid climbing. These are similar features to the earlier electrical model and the later Foster tank. Yet no designs of track accompany his drawings of vehicles. Macfie was tainted by the disputes. In November, he resigned. After publicization of Foster's tank in September 1916, Macfie found financiers. In December, he approached Stern for the necessary steel. Stern requested drawings, but Macfie claimed Stern had not treated his earlier drawings fairly. That was the end of Macfie's official work, although not the recriminations, which culminated in 1919 with false claims by both Macfie and Nesfield to have a stake in Foster's tank (Fletcher 2001: 31; Glanfield 2001: 113-114).

While Macfie was the wrong person to lead a development project, the point is that by mid-April Crompton knew that at least one person was working to improve the Holt track. This helps to explain Crompton's belated attention to alternative tracks, although not his continuing avoidance of British alternatives to Pedrail.

In January, Crompton had rebuffed the agent for Killen-Strait Manufacturing

This official photograph, and others taken on the same ground, on the same day, suggest that the RNAS still needed experience with the Killen-Strait tractor hours before official visitors arrived to see it demonstrated on 30th June 1915.

Company of Wisconsin. In mid-April he accepted the agent's second invitation. Additionally, he belatedly ordered a survey of American tracks in Britain.

The Killen-Strait tractor (see Table 1) was demonstrated on 27th April, by William Strait himself. It was too small to carry more than a machine-gun team, its tracks were no longer than Pedrail's, and they were arranged like an unstable tricycle. Nevertheless, Crompton bought it. Its positive differentiations were partial springing of the running gear, and a sloped track to aid climbing (although only rearwards). He arranged for trials with an added platform to bear test loads, which never happened because the next day he saw a better tractor.

On 28th April, Crompton went to see a Bullock Creeping Grip tractor (see Table 1) in agricultural use in Kent. This looked most like the Foster Centipede, with two wheels at the front, two tracks at the rear. The tracks were the longest and most robust yet seen. (Most tracks were chains of steel frames, linked by pins, to which were bolted wider wooden feet. The Bullock tracks used the largest iron plates yet seen.) Crompton wrote to the agent with an order for two vehicles of the larger type (California Giant, developing 75 bhp instead of 50). He intended to apply both to his articulated design, except he lowered the payload to 30 men (see Table 2).

On 7th May, the Landships Committee authorized purchase of: two California Giants for experimentation in articulated configuration; two sets of longer running gear, each sufficient for a longer chassis (4 feet 8 inches longer), to be assembled in Britain as the Self-Moving Cupola Mark IIa; and completion of the Pedrail vehicle to Crompton's latest specifications (Mark II) (see Table 2). Bullock promised the new running gear within four months of receipt of drawings. Crompton sent an assistant (George Field) as his liaison (Fletcher 2001: 32-33; Glanfield 2001; 84-87).

The Bullock Creeping Grip's observers had been Crompton, Hetherington, Legros, Stern, and a man who should have been involved from the start. Walter Gordon Wilson was a peacetime designer of aircraft, cars, and trucks. Before that he had served as a naval officer. He was currently serving as a technician with the RNAS (since December). Crompton set Wilson to design the linkages between the two articulated vehicles. Steering would be achieved via hydrualic rams (forcing the vehicles apart on one side more than the other). Cables – tensioned by winches – would allow one vehicle to raise the front of the other to help it cross gaps, steps, and slopes. Wilson doubted whether the requirement justified such complications, but completed the drawings on 25th May.

Crompton had no doubts. On 20th May, he wrote to D'Eyncourt of the "increasing importance" of "[auto]moving forts" or "landships" carrying infantrymen and grenade-throwers within range of enemy trenches. He estimated that landships could achieve – at one-tenth the cost in ammunitions and lives – what indirect fire was currently doing. He was writing to repeat his wish to be put in front of the commander of the BEF. At last Crompton wanted to meet the Army's requirements, although he still did not get them right (Glanfield 2001: 90-91).

Consolidating efforts

The Army had the right ideas from the bottom up but not the urgency from the top down. The Admiralty had the urgency without the right ideas. The two ministries were not co-operating because the Army knew itself as the only user of tracked tractors, while Churchill wanted to keep tracked AFVs to himself.

Fortunately, Churchill was on his way out. Since February, the Admiralty was preoccupied with naval and amphibious operations against the Dardanelles in Turkey. These bogged down by May. The First Sea Lord (the highest uniformed authority in the Admiralty) emotionally resigned on 15th May after failing to influence Churchill. The remaining Sea Lords made clear they would not serve him. Churchill offered his resignation on 21st May. On the 25th, Asquith brought opposition parties into a coalition government. The Conservative Party's only condition was that Churchill must leave the Admiralty. Asquith demoted Churchill to the non-executive position of Chancellor of the Duchy of Lancaster. His successor, Arthur Balfour (1848-1930), a former Conservative prime minister, permitted him to stay on the Landships Committee, while the Admiralty sought to divest it.

The War Office did not find out directly. In late May, one of its liaisons to the BEF (Captain Ralph Glyn) visited the Admiralty to confirm hearsay that Crompton *et al* were desperately sourcing materials and technologies for tracked vehicles. On 30th May, one of the Sea Lords informed Scott-Moncrieff of the landships. Through him, Scott-Moncrieff and Glyn visited D'Eyncourt, who showed the plans of Crompton's Mark IIa. They then visited Crompton, who begged for help.

When the Landships Committee met on 8th June, Churchill lifted his ban on contact with the War Office, and thus permitted the Committee to ask the WO to specify the Landship's armaments and obstacle-crossing capabilities (Stern 1919: 22-24). On 10th June, Scott-Moncrieff naively told the MGO that the Admiralty appeared to have solved the problems that Holden had treated as insurmountable

The two California Giants are displayed for the first time with their mirrored gear for articulating, steering, and winching up the fronts. Wilson stands at right.

in February. The MGO agreed to form an inter-ministerial Landships Committee, although he waited until 21st June before formally inviting the Admiralty.

The MGO (Donop) must have been waiting on a requirement from the BEF. The requirement was triggered independently by Swinton, who had remained ignorant of any development of tracked fighting vehicles. On 1st June, he submitted to the BEF's commander (John French) a paper setting the case for "Armoured Machine-Gun Destroyers." French forwarded this to his Engineer-in-Chief (Major-General George Fowke), who expanded on his reply of October: tracked vehicles were too heavy for the bridges, too slow for battle, too tall to hide, and too difficult to develop. Their back-and-forth lasted until 19th June, when Swinton returned to London to cover for Hankey's travel overseas. GHQ formed an Experiments Committee, some of whose members had already sympathized with Swinton. They recommended that an experienced supplier of automobiles should comment. On 22nd June, French sent Swinton's paper to the War Office with recommendation to engage automobile suppliers in experimentation (Swinton 1932: 163).

The WO appointed four of its own to the Landships Committee: Scott-Moncrieff, Holden, the Director of Staff Duties (in charge of Army requirements: Colonel W.D. Bird), and the head of the General Staff's artillery branch (Major E.L. Wheeler). D'Eyncourt remained chairman, but protected the navy and himself by spending more time on ship-building. This left Churchill (still the Committee's only minister) holding the chair at the first inter-ministerial meeting on 29th June (Churchill 1923: 73; Harris 1995: 17-20, 24-25; Glanfield 2001: 96-100).

The Armoured Car Division of the RNAS was absorbed by the Army, except 50 experimental personnel, retained as 20th Squadron, at Wormwood Scrubs in West London. Their chief (Wing Commander Frederick Boothby) joined the Landships Committee in time for its meeting of 8th June. Stern became Secretary on 16th June.

Churchill deflected blame by circulating a paper on 18th June condemning the lack of solution to the "problem of crossing two or three hundred yards of open ground and of traversing and destroying barbed wire...[It] ought not to be beyond the range of modern science if sufficient authority had backed the investigation."

Still Churchill obstructed the War Office. He persuaded the new Minister of Munitions (David Lloyd George) to take over 20th Squadron.

On 30th June, the 20th Squadron demonstrated current projects to ministers and principals from the Ministry of Munitions, War Office, and Landships Committee. Hetherington demonstrated the Killen-Strait tractor with a wire cutter, but it lacked the power to push through or pull out a thin array of wire. Later in the day, the RNAS showed it with an armored body (otherwise used on a Delauney-Belleville touring car). This body had been prepared since May, on the orders of Boothby, following a visit to RNAS armored cars in the roadless area near the Dardanelles. Thus, the Killen-Strait became the first armored tracked vehicle. Yet it never received the turret and thus was not the first armed tracked vehicle. It was soon converted back to a tractor, and transferred with Boothby to an airship station.

The only other automobile on display was a venerable Rolls-Royce Armored Car, which remained the principal type in all three services for more than 20 years. It was superior to the Killen-Strait except in off-road tractive effort.

A pushable Pedrail tracked carriage was demonstrated, with a model shield made from wood. It was not much to show for 10 months of urgent drive, as Churchill characterized his efforts. The products were parochial and no use on the main front of the war (Fletcher 2001: 36-37; Glanfield 2001: 101-102). Nevertheless,

On 30th June 1915, Hetherington drives the Killen-Strait tractor over some timber (above) and, later, into some desultory barbed wire (below). From right to left can be seen David Lloyd George, General Scott-Moncrieff, Churchill, and Colonel Bird.

The Killen-Strait returns with a body from a Delauney-Belleville armored car.

Lloyd George repeated Churchill's myth that they were steps to the tank, and that the Admiralty developed the tank (Lloyd George 1938: 382). Lloyd George wrote this more than two decades later, when both men were in the political wilderness and seeking some ethos with which to intervene in Britain's rearmament.

The Ministry had already taken from the MGO the Royal Ordnance Factories, including their Inventions Branch. Thus, the War Office lost control of research, contracting, production, inspections (of suppliers), and acceptances (of supplies). The WO nominally retained requirements, specifications, design, and development, but practically these things remained scattered over three ministries, dozens of lead contractors, BEF GHQ, and (most neglected) the arms and branches.

Most of the Ministry's employees were soldiers, but they could not take orders from or give reports to the War Office without the Ministry's say-so. Most activities relating to tanks fell under the Ministry's Department for Trench Warfare. Jackson took command of this, which was meritorious, but denuded the War Office of its first in-house champion of amored tracked vehicles.

In early August, 20th Squadron moved five miles north to the new Department for Trench Warfare's testing ground at Wembley Park, where its 50 naval personnel became soldiers. The Army supplied another 550 men. The War Office specified the tests, but could not enforce anything (Williams-Ellis 1920: 10). In July, Lloyd George elevated the Inventions Branch to Department, under a civilian, who took less notice of the War Office. The MGO wrote a telling letter on 19th October:

> I view with dismay the manner in which this subject is being dealt with. A War Office committee was appointed for it, the CID is also dealing with it, a conference decides on what should be done, they are called Admiralty Landships, the personnel is to come from a naval organisation[,] and I am asked for the provision of guns and ammunition[,] the patterns of which I have not been consulted.

Lloyd George characterized Donop as obstructive, and ordered the Ministry's ordnance officers to sever links (even though most were soldiers) (1938: 370-373).

The Admiralty ceded the Landships Committee to the Ministry of Munitions on 17th July. The MGO did not follow suit until 17th August, the Army Council until 25th November. The Committee would continue to report to D'Eyncourt (at the Admiralty), until he saw fit to rule the first product satisfactory, when the Department for Inventions would take sole charge. (This would occur in February.)

Given the routine absence of D'Eyncourt, Churchill dominated the Committee, until he left the government in November (when the coalition closed operations in Turkey). This explains why the Committee's legacy programs persisted, at the same time as Foster developed the eventual tank, with no help from the Committee.

Lingering big wheels

On 16th May 1915, Tritton showed a wooden mock-up of the Foster Trench Tractor. He had added a second deck, to accommodate the 70 passengers, and shortened the trailer to keep the weight the same. Only Hetherington and Wilson attended. Within a few days, Hetherington called in Tritton, to say that the extra height prevented the machine-gun from firing to the flanks, and would foul cables and other obstructions along the roads to the front. The other attendees, including Crompton, Legros, Wilson, Stern, and their armor officer, wondered if the trailer could be pushed so that the machine-gun faced forward – but then it could not be steered. Tritton suggested the trailer could be towed on to the battlefield, then decoupled to move about on electrical power, supplied via cable from the tractor. The RNAS officers excitedly discussed silent approaches at night, with increased payloads, and even explosives for sacrificial detonation against the target.

They asked Tritton to put his idea in writing. On 5th June, Tritton wrote to Crompton that he was abandoning the Trench Tractor in favor of a smaller four-wheeled "armoured wagon or fort," in two versions. One could be electrically powered from another vehicle, as it played out a cable a mile long, into a ploughed 1-foot ditch. The other would be powered by a Daimler Silent Knight engine, with less room for passengers, but lighter base weight (by 4 long tons; 4.1 metric; 4.5 US). Each would mount a machine-gun at each front corner (Rigby 1919).

Crompton focused his criticisms on the electrical specifications. On this excuse, Churchill cancelled Foster's work at a meeting of the Landships Committee on 8th June. The next day the Foster Portable Bridge Machine was scheduled for demonstration, after which it was converted back to a gun tractor (Pullen 2007: 23).

Separately, on 3rd June, Tritton had drawn a new version of the Portable Bridge Machine with an armored superstructure and a forward-firing machine-gun. In 1918, Tritton claimed that this provoked an order for 70 vehicles, later cancelled. The drawing survives, without any evidence for the order (Glanfield 2001: 90).

Yet stranger projects persisted, without surviving explanations. Hetherington's position on the Landship Committee helps to explain why his 300-ton proposal survived through at least December 1916, when John I. Thorneycroft & Company Limited submitted drawings of several versions.

Lingering Self-Moving Cupolas

Even Crompton's articulated trench-enfilading personnel carrier survived. He secured a new lead contractor (McEwan & Pratt, which had produced gears for the Mark II). Bullock's two California Giants reached the company, in Burton-upon-Trent, on 16th June, albeit rusty, after travelling as deck cargo. Officers from 20th

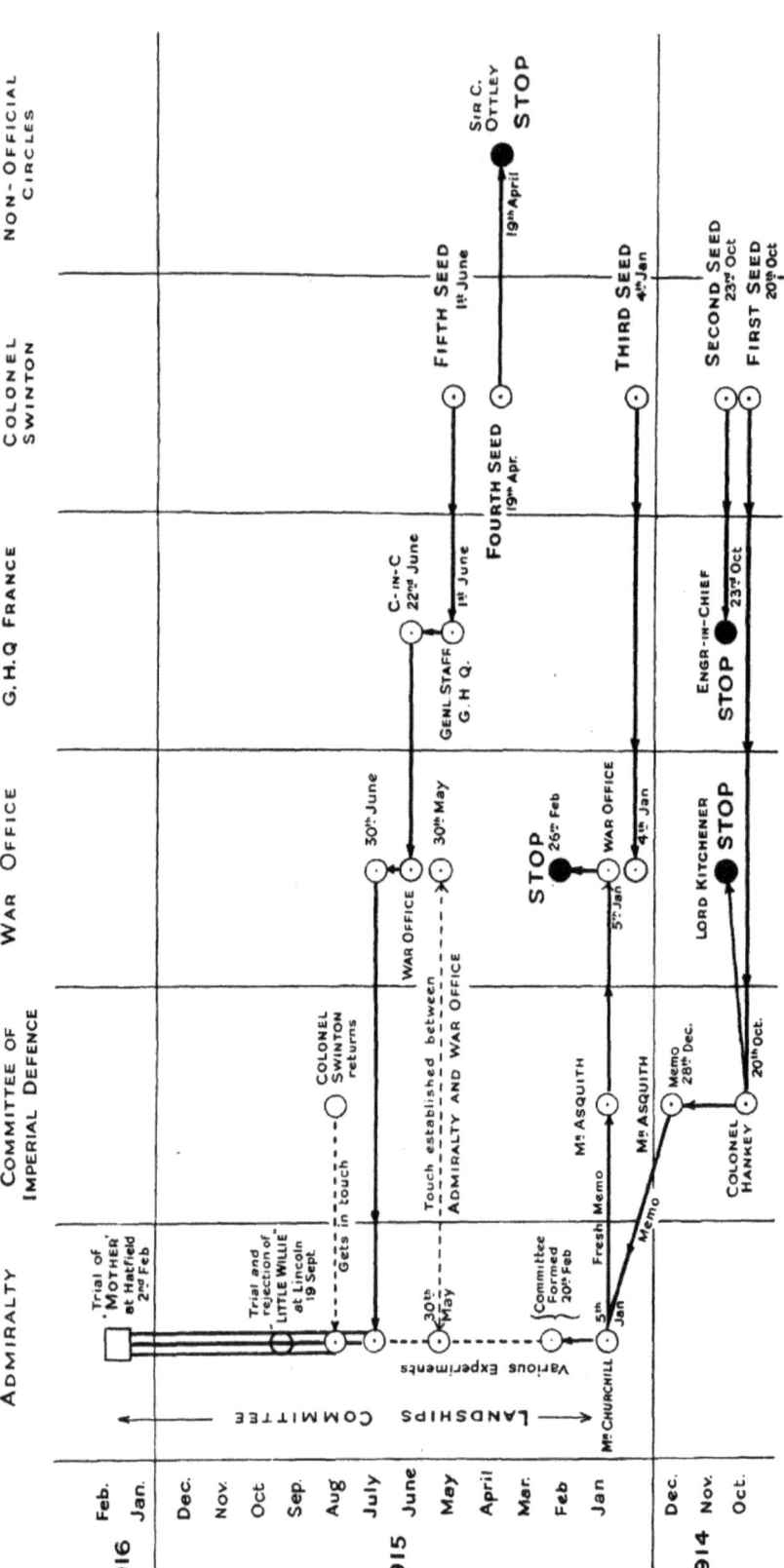

This is how Swinton illustrated the fates of his proposals for a tracked AFV (Swinton 1932: Appendix). Swinton drew an engineer's "fault tree," where the "seeds" are his proposals, and the "stops" are other people's failures to carry them forward. This graphic should not be read as a development tree. The eventual tank's development begins in June 1915, when Swinton's specifications change the Admiralty's requirement and get the War Office and Ministry of Munitions involved. Swinton's schematic inaccurately keeps this under the Admiralty.

Squadron, led by Wilson, articulated them for trials over trenches dug nearby.

The two California Giants, unlike the Creeping Grip Tractor, had the engine at the rear, over the tracks, thus improving drive. The radiator was over the wheels, helping with traction during steering. Nevertheless, they kept getting stuck. Contrary to Crompton's expectations, one tractor was not able to push or pull the other.

McEwan & Pratt tried one with an external steel frame carrying six vertical wooden poles, footed with wider pieces of wood named "elephant's feet." They were intended to stop the tractor sinking further should any track drop in a trench.

In late July, the tractors were driven 120 miles (193 km) by road to Wembley Park, perhaps as proof of sustainability. This took three weeks, to mid August, when they started more tests, likely as separate tractors (Fletcher 2001: 37-38).

The California Giants were not intended for the Mark IIa. It was awaiting the longer running gear from Bullock, due by mid-September. Crompton could hope that the Mark IIa would perform better, given longer ground contact and the revolutionary transmission linking the efforts of both machines. (The California Giants had been articulated back to front, so that one was driving forward while the other was reversing. However, no forward speed matched the reverse speed.)

By June, Crompton was on borrowed time. Churchill was still desperate for him to succeed, which would have vindicated both men. Crompton and Legros had their contracts extended through August. However, Stern curbed Crompton for making orders beyond authority, although Stern became a hypocrite on this issue.

Stern was promoted to Secretary on the same day as Scott-Moncrieff sent the War Office's first specification of a tracked AFV (16th June). He wrote as "we," a conventional short-hand for the General Staff, particuarly the DSD, who was Glyn's boss. Glyn must have carried Swinton's specifications of 1st June: a 40-mm two-pounder automatic cannon ("Pom Pom"), two machine-guns, protection against German steel-cored bullets, caterpillar tracks, speed of 4 mph, and ability to cross trenches 4 feet (1.2 m) wide and steps 5 feet (1.5 m) tall. On 16th June, Scott-Moncrieff specified the two cannons side-by-side towards the front, the two machine-guns behind, firing predominantly sideways, perhaps from turrets ("on the lines of the broadside fire of ships") (see Table 2).

The tandem Bullock California Giants start trials, with the front of one held off the ground.

In August 1916, the Pedrail chassis is parked against a revetment, proving its hopeless prospects for climbing anything.

Boothby agitated for a mix of six wheels and track units on a single vehicle. He possibly carried forward that number after thinking of two articulated Killen-Strait tractors, although he now opposed articulated vehicles. He was not replying to the War Office: he wrote to Crompton. D'Eyncourt removed Boothby for challenging his authority and interfering with design.

On 2nd July, the Landships Committee reclassified the "self-moving cupola" as "caterpillar machine-gun destroyer," to Swinton's specifications. Scott-Moncrieff added that the General Staff preferred six 40-mm cannons, four machine-guns, and 25 men. Crompton designed a Mark III, with four turrets, two on each vehicle. Each end turret was lower, so that the turret behind could fire over. He placed a machine-gun in each corner of the front hull (see Table 2). Crompton told one of the founders of the Machine-Gun Corps (George Lindsay), the prospective user, that 75-mm guns could be mounted. This explains why the eventual tank was modeled with a 40-mm cannon and a 75-mm gun on respective sides (Fletcher 2001: 38).

In the second week of July, Stern asked Wilson whether he would rather work on the project with Crompton or Tritton. Wilson replied: "If Tritton and I are put on the job we would soon produce a machine that could do something."

D'Eyncourt took Tritton to pick up blueprints on 15th July, but Crompton promised drawings by the end of the month. On 19th July, Rigby arrived as a sort of reviewer (Rigby to Fletcher, 18th May 1967). Rigby returned to Foster on 24th July with what Tritton reported as "a mere sketch." "We have no instructions, drawings, nor details as to the various mechanisms we have to incorporate."

Unknown to Crompton, on 21st July, Stern warned Tritton to prepare to build 12 landships. The next day, the Committee met. Crompton argued for production of the Mark III. Instead, it ordered Foster to prove Bullock's longer running gear on one chassis before a decision on the complete Mark III. Crompton was ordered to design steering for independent chassis. He added two wheels at the back, with Ackerman linkages. No production drawings reached Foster, so, on 30th July Stern told Tritton that Crompton would be cut out. On 6th August, Crompton and Legros received notice from D'Eyncourt that their contracts would not be renewed, they should stop making orders, and they should pass everything to Foster.

Crompton and Legros served out their time by redesigning the Mark III, without the upper turrets, to save weight and height (Mark IIIa). In mid-August, Field returned from America, seconding Boothby's preference for a single vehicle with Killen-Strait running gear (given its slope). Crompton and Legros then designed an even lighter and shorter vehicle on the Killen-Strait chassis (Mark IV) (see Table 2). Crompton ruined whatever credit he deserves by denigrating Foster's tank as inferior (Fletcher 2001: 38-39; Glanfield 2001: 93-97, 102-105, 109).

Crompton's preferences were disproven within a year. On 7th June, Tulloch wrote to Jackson, bemoaning German technological leadership, and reasserting his proposal of January. Jackson sponsored an AFV to carry a large flamethrower his department was developing. In early July, the lead contractor for Crompton's Mark II stopped work for the third time, after demanding more compensation and less inspection. Crompton kept persuading the Admiralty to concede because he thought Metropolitan Carriage, Wagon, & Finance was the only company with suitable presses to make Pedrail tracks, but he had not thoroughly researched the matter, and Diplock had not finished drawings. The WO persuaded the Admiralty to cancel the contract, then found a new lead contractor (Stothert & Pitt of Bath). Everything needed months of further development. Stothert & Pitt designed a rigid chassis, like Crompton's Mark I. In May 1916, it was reallocated as a tractor. It was driven out on 7th June, but barely managed to climb a step of 4 inches (102 mm). Trials waited until August, and ended with failures in the Pedrail units (Harris 1995: 23-24; Fletcher 2001: 35; Glanfield 2001: 114-115).

Number 1 Lincoln Machine (Little Willie)

Foster was left with the warning order of 30th July to design and develop an unarticulated AFV, using the longer Bullock running gear. Legros was carried over, but soon dropped out. Wilson was appointed Superintendent. Whatever Tritton's faults in dealing with Crompton and Legros, he showed no egotism with Wilson. Tritton's commercial experience complemented Wilson's practical experience. Their creative tension was productive (Fletcher 2001: 40; Glanfield 2001: 118).

The Number 1 Lincoln Machine, with its dummy turret hidden by canvas, is tried on Cross O'Cliff Hill, outside Lincoln, on 19th September, after modification of the running gear to give more rise.

Bullock delivered the longer running gear early: the parts landed in Liverpool on 3rd August. The Landships Committee specified a vehicle that could carry a 40-mm cannon and a machine-gun in a revolving turret over a 5-foot gap, a 4.5-foot step, and boggy ground. Otherwise, its members made clear, as Rigby paraphrased them, "that, as they as a body did not seem to make much headway, entire freedom to design and build a machine should be given to Sir W.A. Tritton and his technical staff at Messrs. Foster & Co." (Rigby 1919; Butler 1926: 3) On 15th August, Foster logged, in five words, an order for construction of a landship (Pullen 2007: 27).

Tritton and Wilson designed a hull slightly longer than the gear, and a dummy turret almost as wide as the hull. The turret was never designed to rotate; its vertical space was partly filled by the engine, at the rear, and the drive to the front. On 3rd September, Stern suggested it should slide forwards on rails to give line of fire on targets close ahead. After the first trial, it was removed, then the upper hole was plated over, leaving apertures in the sides as the only means for firing from within.

Foster started construction on 11th August. Days later, Wilson added a wheeled tail to improve steering and trench crossing. Tritton wisely added brakes on the drives to the tracks. The Number 1 Lincoln Machine ran on 9th September, when Wilson and Tritton modified the running gear to give more rise at front and back, to aid steering. On the 19th, it was demonstrated across country to the principals.

Swinton was present, with little thanks to any of the War Office, Admiralty, or BEF. Hankey had tried to get Swinton on the BEF's Experiments Committee, then recalled him to serve as his immediate deputy (Senior Assistant Secretary). This was on 18th July. A week later, he visited Kitchener at the War Office, on committee business, but neither man raised landships. On 30th July, he visited D'Eyncourt, who directed him to Stern. According to Stern, their conversation went like this:

> "Lieutenant Stern, this is the most extraordinary thing I have ever seen. The Director of Naval Construction appears to be making land battleships for the Army who have never asked for them and are doing nothing to help. You have nothing but naval ratings doing all your work. What on earth are you? Are you a mechanic or a chauffeur?"
> "A banker."
> "This makes it still more mysterious." (Stern 1919: 41-42)

Stern invited him to observe the first demonstration of the Number 1 Lincoln Machine, after which he took increasing responsibility for liaising with the WO.

On the day, the tracks disengaged while traversing slopes and trenches, and eventually sheared the flanges off the rollers. This was a problem seen on Bullock tractors, now exacerbated by longer tracks. Rigby blamed sideways play in the pins, while Field blamed Tritton for not fitting Bullock's bracing members. The vehicle took two days to get to the workshop, where rollers of tougher steel were tried, without satisfaction (Rigby 1919; Fletcher 2001: 41; Glanfield 2001: 118).

Centipede (Big Willie)

Wilson and Tritton already realized how to improve the gear, but not yet the track. On 17th August, Wilson had suggested to Tritton that tracks could run around the hull, and that the armament could move to side sponsons. In the next week, Tritton promised D'Eyncourt mobility equivalent to a wheel 50 feet (15 m) in diameter, which became the justification for the War Office to issue a new trench-crossing specification on 26th August: 8 feet (2.4 m). D'Eyncourt authorized

A Bullock Creeping Grip's track disengages from its rollers over a trench, in April 1915.

a new vehicle, which Tritton named after his semi-tracked "Centipede" of 1913.

A wooden model was ready to show the principals on 19th September, but the tracks were still in the research stage. Tritton considered how to reinforce conveyor belts made of cotton and Balata rubber, before wheeling back to steel and a revolutionary design. His joy comes across in a telegram sent to Stern on 22nd September:

> Balata died on test bench yesterday morning STOP New arrival by Tritton out of pressed plate STOP Light in weight but very strong STOP All doing well, thank you STOP [signed] Proud parents

The plate was pressed with a lip at one end, rivetted to a casting that would accommodate the pin that linked two plates together. Flanges rivetted on the inside would engage iron rails so that the tracks could not drop away when crossing a hollow. The disadvantage was that engagement with the rails constrained the track's inherent suspension. In theory, the rails or rollers could be sprung, but that would have taken internal space or added external width.

According to Rigby, "Wilson designed the outer shape," Tritton the tracks, and Tritton and Rigby the automotive line (Rigby to David Fletcher, 18th May 1967). The full-scale wooden model was adjusted, then sent by lorry to Wembley Park, where it was viewed on 29th September by principals from the Admiralty, War Office, Ministry of Munitions, BEF, and CID (Swinton). The authorities were happy, except to reassert their specification for a speed of 4 mph (Wilson had adopted the speed achieved on Little Willie: 2 mph). The armament was mounted in sponsons that could be removed from each side to stay within the railway loading width. The model showed a 40-mm cannon on one side, a 2.95-inch (75 mm) mountain gun/howitzer on the other, but both were in short supply. In December, they would be replaced with 57-mm six-pounders, from Admiralty stocks.

Little Willie is displayed with new running gear, which carried forward to Medium A.

Otherwise, Foster waited on armor. The new type of track was tested on the bench on 22nd November. The new running gear was proven on Little Willie on 8th December (Fletcher 2001: 42-44; Glanfield 2001: 120-121; Pullen 2007: 153).

Construction of the new vehicle started on 29th October. At different times it was known as "Centipede," "The Wilson," "Big Willie" or "Mother." Swinton still referred to it as the "Land Cruiser." The company disguised the automotive system as a "demonstration and instruction chassis" for the Royal Marines, the hull as a "water carrier for Mesopotamia" (Rigby 1919; Butler 1926: 4-5). In 1923, Rigby recalled that "due to frequent modifications to Mother's hull the water carrier soon became known around the foundry as that bloody water tank, soon to be simplified to tank" (Pullen 2007: 153).

The pilot first moved under its own power on 7th January 1916. Several track plates fractured, so all plates were tempered locally. On 12th January, it drove out again, and over some scrap in the yard. The next day it moved to Foster's proving ground. On the 19th, Hetherington and Stern came up to fire some shot into the ground, to see how the superstructure handled the shock. On the 27th, the WO specified trials of "the Tank," then the Ministry of Munitions printed a schedule for a "Tank Trial" (Rigby 1919; Lloyd George 1938: 385). "Mother" was entrained on 28th January to private grounds at Hatfield Park. (Wembley Park was rejected as too public.) On 2nd February, it was demonstrated to the political heads of the War Office, Admiralty, and Ministry of Munitions, and their staff. Kitchener left early, after saying that such a "pretty mechanical toy" would be easily knocked out by artillery. Nevertheless, his CIGS and the Admiralty's head were most enthused.

> The experiment was a complete success, the tank achieving even more than it was asked to accomplish. And I can recall the feeling of delighted amazement with which I saw for the first time the ungainly monster, bearing the inscription "H.M.S. Centipede" on its breast, plough through thick entanglements, wallow through deep mud, and heave its huge bulk over parapets and across trenches. At last, I thought, we have the answer to the German machine-guns and wire. Mr. Balfour's delight was as great as my own, and it was only with difficulty that some of us persuaded him to disembark from H.M. Landship, whilst she crossed the last test, a

trench several feet wide. (Lloyd George 1938: 383)

Balfour's enthusiasm is confirmed by Rigby:

> Mr. Balfour seemed more interested than the others in the working of the machine from the inside. It was with difficulty that he was persuaded to come out when the machine was to be tried over an obstacle hitherto unattempted. (Rigby 1919)

Nevertheless, Rigby recalls, "The opinions expressed after the trials were very non-committal." Rigby thus refutes Lloyd George's later claim to have been enthusiastic from the start. Indeed, Mother stayed on trial for weeks. The King attended another demonstration on 8th February, by when Mother had been running for 28 days. On 12th February, the War Office formally requested 100 "Mark I Heavy Tanks," with some modifications from Big Willie. On the same day, Lloyd George asked Stern to lead a Tank Supply Committee (later: the Mechanical Warfare Supply Department). By its second meeting (28th February), he had reached agreement with Foster and Metropolitan Carriage for production, although Wilson warned of further development of the engine-cooling radiator, hydraulic controls, steering tail, ammunition stowage, and loopholes. Deliveries started in July. They fought first at Flers-Courcelette, on 15th September 1916.

Why was Britain first?

Britain was advantaged by its mature engineering capacities and familiarity with American capacities. These capacities were not utilized as early as they could have been, because a few people held the right authorities but the wrong ideas.

The first people to blame are soldiers. In the War Office, Holden and Donop are most to blame for curbing tracked trials before the First World War (1905-1911), and reacting slowly and unambitiously to requirements during the war (August 1914 to February 1915). Lest we under-estimate their authorities, remember that Holden was President of the Military Transport Committee before the war, and Assistant Director of Mechanical Transport Supply during war, while Donop became the Director of Artillery in 1911, and the Master General of Ordnance in 1913.

In France, the BEF's commander (John French) and chief engineer (George Fowke) were slow to realize Ernest Swinton's requirement (October 1914 to June 1915). The army itself cannot be blamed: in November 1914, middling officers spun off a Motor Machine-Gun Service, which would become the first user of tanks.

In the first year of war, the Admiralty was investing most in AFVs, although not in tanks. From October 1914 to June 1915, Winston Churchill wasted colossal

Mother is posed for its first official photographs.

resources on the wrong requirements (bridge-layer, trench-enfilading personnel carrier, big wheel landship, pushable shield). His quick memoirs (masquerading as histories) mischaracterized these things as "tanks," and spun "landship" as a synonym for tank. In fact, he had formed the Landships Committee (in February 1915) to focus on trench-enfilading personnel carriers and big wheel landships. This was after less dogmatic heads (such as Sueter) switched requirements to what we now know as tanks (tracked vehicles with firearms in turrets). None of Churchill's efforts necessarily contributed to the tank. Most delayed the tank.

The decisive period was from late May 1915, when Churchill was demoted, and the Admiralty revealed its Landships program to the War Office, to late June, when the WO appointed its own staff to the Committee, and redirected the requirement away from a personnel carrier, with little armament or battlefield mobility, to an artillery-armed, trench-crossing "machine-gun destroyer."

The War Office, thanks mostly to Swinton, got the requirement right in June 1915, but still needed to design and develop something that fulfilled that requirement. What it inherited from the Admiralty proved unsuitable. The Admiralty had chosen the wrong people to design tracked vehicles, from its Air Division down through the RNAS to the armored car force. None of its personnel had experience with tracks, except Macfie. Macfie's insistence on tracks did not divert the wheeled efforts, until February, when Sueter belatedly agreed. Sueter, however, naively chose Pedrail tracks. He also sponsored Macfie to develop a new tracked vehicle, but Macfie never proved new tracks, and got into a professional tangle to boot.

Churchill had appointed the Landships Committee with three other members. None had experience with tracks. They engaged Crompton as chief designer, whose experience with tracks was vicarious and negative (through Holden). He embraced Churchill's trench-enfilading personnel carrier. Like Sueter, he reacted to Macfie's advocacy of Holt tracks by adopting Pedrail tracks, given a conflict of interest since his pre-war partnership with Diplock. Crompton under-estimated Diplock's unreliability, and over-estimated his own competencies, even though his specialty was electrical. He persisted with articulated tandem Pedrail tracks, without researching the alternatives, battlefield, or user requirements, until April 1915.

The Admiralty never produced anything tracked, except a mock shield on a pushable Pedrail carriage (June 1915). The only tracked automobile with roots in an Admiralty project was a Pedrail chassis finished by the War Office, after another

Mother is proven in Lincoln, circa 14th January 1916.

year of work (June 1916). This was taken over initially as a self-propelled flame-thrower, finally as a transport vehicle. It failed even its reduced role. Crompton had chosen the wrong tracks (Pedrail), the wrong configuration (articulated tandem running gears), and the wrong corner of the capability triangle (survivability – via lowness to the ground – at the expense of mobility and lethality).

Foster developed the tank (August 1915 to January 1916) on a contract initiated by the WO. The Admiralty had wasted Foster on wheeled vehicles. Foster's prior work on tracks (1913) was never utilized by any military. The only material carried over from Crompton's work to Foster was Bullock's longer running gear. This was not necessary to the tank, although it might have been necessary to Tritton's and Wilson's realization of a revolutionary running gear in September 1915.

This is the most telling period. From August 1915 to January 1916, the tank was contracted, specified, designed, developed, piloted, and tried (see Table 3), despite increasing structural tensions between Ministry of Munitions, Admiralty, and War Office. By then, Tritton and Wilson had accumulated a year's experience with war-time acquisitions, and were acting mostly autonomously. Almost everything they did was approved as presented. They were further vindicated by acceptance of the pilot tank with little further development. They were enabled by Stern, who, as first administrator and then Secretary of the Landships Committee, shielded them from inter-ministerial jostling and contradictions, as Tritton later acknowledged:

> I have no words to express my feelings at the generous way in which the British Government have treated the designers and originators of the tank. The friendly relationship which has prevailed between your good self and all of us at Lincoln since March 1915 will always remain a pleas-ant memory. (Tritton to Stern, 21st November 1917, RACTM)

Now, let us think of how much earlier the British could have delivered tanks if the War Office had acted on the first requirement, and if the Admiralty had not wasted 22 months on the wrong concepts. It wasted four months on wheeled bridge-layers and big-wheeled gunships (October 1914 to February 1915). The Pedrail chassis was not delivered until 16 months after Crompton had specified it. Two months later, it was condemned (see Table 3).

By contrast, the real tank project lasted five to seven months. Foster was made lead contractor in August, and delivered Mother just over five months later. Crompton had taken a couple weeks to research tracks (April-May 1915), before ordering longer Bullock tracks, which took more than a month to arrive (May-June 1915). Thus, this track research and development period comes to less than two months. If Tritton and Wilson might have revolutionized track design without Bull-ock tracks, the necessary period for the tank's design and development falls from seven to five months.

If Swinton's requirement had been taken as seriously in October 1914 as in June 1915, the tank could have been delivered around the cusp of March/April 1915, or May/June if we include the Bullock tracks. Perhaps it could have been delivered in 1912, if Tulloch had been taken seriously in 1911.

These estimates are for the tank as materially delivered. An armored Holt could have been made quicker, by early 1915, if the War Office had sponsored Macfie's suggestion of August 1914, or Swinton's of October. This estimate becomes clearer in the next chapter, which describes the other national tank users of the Great War.

Country	Side	First requirement	Specification	Pilot	First operational use	Time specification to pilot	Time specification to use	Explanations
Britain	Western Allies	November 1911 (Tulloch); August 1914 (Macfie); October 1914 (Swinton); June 1915 (BEF and War Office)	October 1914 to June 1915 (Swinton); 16th June to 26th August 1915 (War Office)	9th to 19th September 1915 (Little Willie); 7th to 12th January 1916 (Big Willie); June-August 1916 (Pedrail chassis)	15th September 1916	5 months (Big Willie only) or 7 months (counting Bullock tracks)	13 months (Big Willie to Mark I)	Superior engineering capacities and bottom-up requirements overcame unambitious War Office and BEF and misdirected Admiralty
France	Western Allies	August 1914 (Estienne); November 1914 (Quellennec); January to May 1915 (Schneider)	January to May 1915 (Schneider); January 1916 (St. Chamond)	9th December 1915 (Schneider Baby Holt); 17th February 1916 (Type A); 17th March (Type C); April (St. Chamond)	16th April 1917	7-11 months (Schneider Baby Holt); 9-13 months (Type A); 10-14 months (Type C); 3 months (St. Chamond)	20-25 months (Schneider); 15 months (St. Chamond)	Similar disconnect from field to government; inferior tractor industry; inferior public-private partnership
Germany	Central Powers	September 1916 (High Command)	September 1916	30th April 1917 (chassis); Sept. 1917 (tank)	21st March 1918	7 months (chassis); 12 months (tank)	18 months (tank)	Low requirement, small automotive sector, high ambition
USA	Western Allies	April 1917 (upon entry into war)	November 1917 (recommendation); February 1918 (receipt French plans)	October 1918 (M1917)	(12th September 1918, with French lights; 29th, with British heavies)	11 months (M1917)	12 months (M1917)	Capacities wasted by unmeritorious cavalry and artillery officers given too much say in the field
Russia	Allies until 1917	-	-	(August 1915, big tricycle)	(Spring 1918, French lights; White Russia)	-	-	Low industrial capacity, foreign supplies, weak requirement
Italy	Western Allies from 1915	October 1916	October 1916	June 1917 (chassis); February 1918 (Fiat 2000)	Spring 1918 at home; 1919 in Libya	16 months	c. 20 months	Stagnation and Allied inspiration overcame low requirement on a mountainous front
Canada	Western Allies	(March 1918, 1st Tank Battalion)	-	-	(March 1919 intended)	-	-	British tank supply; low home personnel supply
New Zealand	Western Allies	(March 1918, one unit programmed)	-	-	(March 1919 intended)	-	-	British tank supply; low home personnel supply
Austro-Hungary	Central Powers	-	-	-	-	-	-	Low requirement given terrain
Turkey	Central Powers	-	-	-	-	-	-	Low requirement given terrain

Table 3: Time taken to procure and deploy tanks during the Great War (sources as per main body text).

CHAPTER 2

Why the rest were next

This chapter explains the belligerents that followed Britain in acquiring tanks during the Great War. As Table 3 summarizes, five states piloted tanks of their own design, of which four used their own designs, before the end of the war. Britain was first. France deployed second (1917), and went on to acquire the most tanks, tank personnel, and tank units of the war (see Table 4). Germany deployed captured British tanks in 1917, followed by a few of its own design in 1918. Its allies used none. The United States (US) was fourth to deploy tank units, and acquired the third largest force before the armistice, although not yet with American tanks. Italy was fourth to deploy tanks of its own design, although in fewest number. Russians used none until "White" anti-revolutionaries received French and British tanks (1918-1919). Canada and New Zealand had programmed units for use in 1919, with British tanks. The other belligerents never programmed any.

France

France had similar advantages to Britain. It was highly industrialized (although Germany's partial occupation of the country would lower its capacity: see Table 4). It had the second largest automobile sector in Europe, behind Britain, ahead of Germany. Its army was the largest in the West. Its requirements for automobiles were stronger, given a long land border with a peer competitor (Germany), which had defeated France as recently as 1871. Automobiles were useful in vast colonies too.

In 1898, the French Army purchased its first petrol-engined vehicle (a Decauville staff car). A machine-gun armed (but unarmored) car was procured in 1906, and deployed against dissident Moroccan tribesmen in 1907. The Army subsequently procured different petrol-engined cars for carrying mail, pigeons, and telegraph equipment. "The French Army in the early 1900s was the most mechanized arm of all the major nations." (Bishop and Ellis 1979: 13)

Nevertheless, the French Army held proportionally fewer automobiles than the British (which was smaller, after all). At the start of the Great War, it deployed 220, all wheeled (91 lorries, 50 Chatillon-Panhard tractors, 46 cars, 31 ambulances, 2 self-propelled guns). One explanation is that the French Army had call on civilian vehicles, through a subvention scheme (in which private automobile owners were compensated for maintenance of their vehicles, in return for which the Army could recquisition those vehicles in emergency). Reserve officers were indemnified for use of their private cars if mobilized. The French Army acquired 6,000 trucks under this scheme, and recquisitioned another 1,000 buses and 2,000 cars upon the outbreak of the Great War (Bishop and Ellis 1979: 12-14, 18-20). On 7th September 1914, the French Army became the first to transport an infantry division by automobiles, including 600 taxi-cabs requisitioned in Paris (Macksey 1973: 147).

French tracked tractors were on offer, but were inferior in power and traction to British tractors. The military did not deploy any in peacetime. Two Holt 60s were imported into Tunisia in 1911 for agricultural work. Inspired by these, Edmond Francois Lefebvre developed an agricultural tractor with steel wheels, plus tracks

A Schneider tank on operations in 1917.

that could be lowered at the rear. He released this in 1913, and demonstrated it to the Army in July 1914, without earning an order.

Earlier in 1914, a consortium of private engineers approached Schneider & Co. (which had supplied automotive parts for Lefebvre's tractor) to develop Holt-like tractors for agriculture. The youngest was Jacques Quellennec, who entered the Army upon war. Recovering from wounds in late October, he realized a requirement for armored Holts. He sent the idea to Eugène Brillié of Schneider, who appeared doubtful, and was away in Spain for subsequent months. Nevertheless, someone at Schneider admitted the requirement by May (Vauvillier 2014: 18-23).

In January 1915, Schneider's representatives attended the British demonstration of a Holt 75 and a Holt 120, then persuaded the French government to finance the purchase of a Baby Holt 45 and a Holt 75. These arrived in May, when Schneider started to design a lengthened running gear. The requirement was ambiguous. Officially, the financing was for tractors, before Brillié returned from Spain and claimed Quellennec's idea. During the same period a French artillery officer in Tunisia requisitioned the two Holt 60s there for his regiment, as it mobilized to join the home army. In September, the home army ordered 15 Baby Holt 45s as artillery tractors. By then, however, the French preferred to carry artillery on trucks rather than drag them (Ellis and Bishop 1970: 131, 143). The declining French requirement for a tracked tractor helps to explain Schneider's dedication to an armored version.

On 9th December, Schneider demonstrated an armored body on a Baby Holt 45. The Baby Holt 45 was more stable than the Holt 75 (given the latter's extension over a steered wheel), although shorter. On 15th December, the Army ordered ten vehicles of this type. However, in subsequent days the pilot proved unable to cross trenches reliably, so, in January, the Army specified a longer running gear. Since the summer, Schneider had designed a version with seven road wheels each side (instead of the received five). These allowed an extra 30 centimetres (11.8 inches) of chassis. All the company needed was the extra parts.

In January 1916, the Army started to receive the Baby Holt 45s it had ordered in September. It sent one to Schneider. On 2nd February, Schneider used its two Baby

Holt 45s to build a longer chassis (later designated "Machine [*L'appareil*] Number 1 Type A"), with eight road wheels each side. On 17th February, the machine was tested: it crossed trenches 1.75 metres (5 feet 9 inches) wide, more than the War Office specification of June 1915 (5 feet) but less than of 26th August (8 feet). On 25th February, the War Ministry ordered 400 "*tracteurs-chenilles type Schneider & Cie blindés*" ("tracked, armoured tractors, Schneider & Company type"). The body, at least, remained developmental, though Types B (2nd March) and C (17th March).

However, the Army and Schneider broke their partnership. Schneider had patented its running gear with seven road wheels, while the Army took the eight-wheel design (in which it claimed a majority stake) to an Army-owned factory in St. Chamond (*Forges et Aciéries de la Marine et d'Homécourt*; FAMH). That factory eventually developed a larger vehice – known as the Saint Chamond heavy tank.

The public-private tensions help to explain why France came second, despite the same peacetime exposure to Holt tractors, and the same period of realization of requirement. However, these tensions are insufficient to explain why design and development were much slower in France. Schneider did not move as quickly as Foster, or even Foster's predecessors. Schneider was intent on developing Holts from January, and received its own Holts in May, but did not deliver any armored version until December, i.e., eleven months after requirement (see Table 3). The first armored Holt and Little Willie were practically equivalent, but Foster developed something much superior by January, while Schneider was still developing its offering in March. (The St. Chamond tank was piloted in April 1916.)

Yes, public-private tensions could explain Schneider's slowness. On the other hand, Schneider had commercial incentives to hurry, and had been financed by the government since January 1915. Schneider was not as quick or effective as Foster. Foster, after all, had more experience of developing tracked and wheeled tractors.

Production too was slower in France. Schneiders were not delivered until September 1916 (partly because the Army preferred to finance St. Chamond). This was the month when the British first used tanks, after which the French Army got around to forming a user arm (*Artillerie Spéciale*), albeit subordinate to the Artillery.

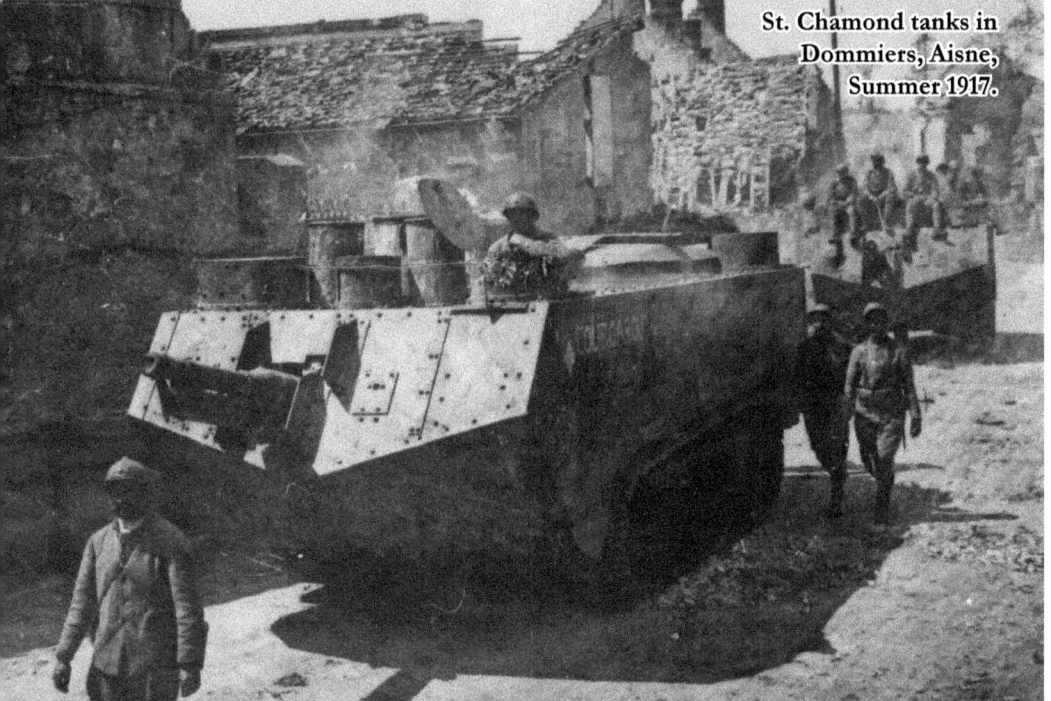

St. Chamond tanks in Dommiers, Aisne, Summer 1917.

A FT with a single 8-mm machine-gun. From March 1918, deliveries were supplemented by a type with a short 37-mm gun.

The commander of the *Artillerie Spéciale* counts as the first French soldier to foresee something like the St. Chamond, although he was not necessary to either the Schneider or the St. Chamond. In late August 1914, Colonel Jean Baptiste Estienne remarked to comrades about the need for an all-terrain self-propelled 75-mm field gun. Estienne discovered Schneider's work in August 1915. His escalations of his requirement were belated and ignored, until December, when he was invited to meet with staff and view Schneider's pilots. He made useful suggestions, but does not count as a designer or developer.

About 200 Schneiders were delivered by 16th April 1917, when the first French tank attack occurred (near Nivelle) – 7 months after the first British tank attack, and 16 months after Schneider ordered Holt tractors. The first St. Chamonds were modified as recovery vehicles, so St. Chamond tanks did not see combat until 5th May. In that month, Schneider production switched to an unarmed carrier version, after 300 tanks. Production of St. Chamonds ended in March 1918, after 377 vehicles. In August, Schneider delivered its 100th carrier. By then, only about 10 Schneider tanks and 72 St. Chamonds were still in service (Chant and Jones 2004: 52).

While the French were not first to develop or deploy heavy or medium tanks, they were first with light tanks. Renault started work on the eventual FT in July 1916, after a second approach from Estienne. Like the British heavy tank, the French light tank synthesized an informed field requirement with industrial expertise.

The FT was piloted in May 1917 and mass-produced from October (see Table 3). Given the cost-effectiveness of this one type, France acquired and deployed the most tanks during the war (see Table 4). France deployed the most automobiles in general. By 1918, the French had almost 70,000 trucks and tractors in military service, more than any other belligerent – equivalent to 35 percent of the trucks fielded by all belligerents (Tucker 2004: 4).

A British Mark IV Heavy is prepared by its German users.

Germany and Austro-Hungary

Before the war, the Central Powers (Germany and Austro-Hungary) acquired automobiles for towing and carrying weapons. Austro-Hungary was best supplied, thanks mainly to Austro-Daimler, despite less industrial capacity overall (see Table 4). Austro-Hungary's army was first (in 1904) to receive an armored car with turret, on a four-wheel-drive truck by Austro-Daimler. In 1914, the Austro-Hungarian government's War Department agreed to assemble Holt tractors under license, although war interrupted the supply of parts from America.

Germany's War Department rejected a Holt 60 demonstrated in 1913, but during war would acquire Holt tractors from Austro-Hungary and Holt's representative. The only German armed, armored vehicles in service were: a self-propelled gun for use against observation balloons (Ehrhardt's *Ballon Abwehr Kanonen*, since 1906); a command/staff car (*Opel Kriegswagen*, since 1906); and another anti-balloon truck by Krupp and Daimler (since 1909). The Army tried the Austro-Daimler armored car in 1905, some French armored cars in 1909 (en route to Russia), and an armored truck carrying a howitzer in 1913. Yet it did not require turreted armored cars until after its northern wing encountered Belgian and British armored cars in August 1914. Heavy armored cars by Büssing, Daimler, and Ehrhardt were issued in 1915, after the end of the mobile period in the West for which they had been required. The Ehrhardt became the predominant acquisition, for the Eastern Front alone (White 1966: 7-8, 18-20; Ellis and Bishop 1970: 125-126).

The Central Powers had less requirement for tanks: they were largely defensive in the West; they led with mountain troops against their southern enemies; and they chased their eastern enemies with horses and cars. The Ottomans relied on railways, horses, and cars, from Turkey to Egypt to Persia.

German intelligence was aware of British "Landships" before first use, perhaps as early as May 1915, when Crompton's desperate procuring became more widely known than intended. In December 1915, a backbencher started asking questions in Parliament. Although journalists were persuaded not to report, his source was not found. From mid-August 1916, British tanks were being demonstrated in France, on ground open to any Allied visitor. German troops received warnings of a new vehicle by September (Fuller 1920: 260; Foley 1963: 15; Glanfield 2001: 123).

However, the High Command did not take the threat seriously until after the first use of tanks on 15th September. Within days, it urgently required an armored assault vehicle (*Sturmpanzerwagen*), thus proving its prior under-estimation. Even then, the Germans were slow to use captured tanks (December 1917). Here, the prompt was an unprecedented penetration of German lines by tanks, at Cambrai, on 20th November. The type (British Mark IV) had been used since 7th June.

Design and development of the first German type was similarly slow. The first chassis was piloted by the War Department's 7th Section (for transport) (*Abteilung 7 (Verkehrswesen)*) on 30th April 1917, more than seven months after requirement. The A7V tank was not piloted until September 1917. The type was not used in combat until 21st March 1918. This was the opening day of an offensive that was supposed to end the war, so maintenance of surprise justified not using the A7Vs earlier. However, only nine tanks were used that day – 6 months since production started, and 18 months since Britain first used tanks (see Table 3). Only 20 A7V tanks were ever delivered (plus 30 of an unarmored carrier variant) (see Table 4).

Germany's enemies preferred prejudicial explanations. For instance, Fuller wrote that "the German…is essentially a stupid (*dumm*) man" (1920: 212, 261).

A contrary explanation is ambition. Like the French, the Germans developed the Holt running gear, but aimed longer. The product would be the largest, best armed, and thickest armored tank deployed during the war – albeit at expense of mobility.

A third explanation is industrial under-capacity. Despite the largest economy in Europe, Germany's automotive capacity was weaker than any of France, Britain, or America. It relied on Austro-Daimler for its heavier requirements. Nevertheless, Germany had the engineers and finance to develop an equivalent heavy automotive capacity if it had wanted (Hundleby and Strasheim 1990: 18-19).

The fourth and best explanation is operational. Germany did not have the same operational needs as its enemies, until it planned a decisive offensive for Spring 1918 (to defeat the Allies in France before the Americans deployed their superior army). Even then, it was satisifed with current arms and dissatisfied with current tanks. This explains why the first tanks it used were Mark IVs, which were easier to drive than the previous Marks it had captured. Its infantry were already faster and more sustainable, and would be lightened for the new offensive (Hundleby and Strasheim 1990: 40, 134, 152-153).

America

The US Army was surprisingly late to mechanize, considering that the country was top in economic size, wealth, industrialization, and automobile production. The Army was small, so should have been easy to mechanize, although a small army justifies a smaller budget, particularly in a country where the Navy is king.

The War Department authorized the Army's first automobile in 1903, but refused the Quartermaster General's order of six more in 1906, leaving him to pay from his personal account. He got another 12 authorized in 1907, but concluded that they were not cost-effective. Up to 1912, the US Army purchased only 28 motorized trucks (Risch 1989: 595-596).

The Army's first tractor was actually procured in the Philippines, in 1909. In 1912, the Field Artillery tried a Holt 60, without order. The Army rebuffed Holt's

"Siegfried" was one of the first nine A7Vs, all used on 31st March 1918.

offer of a further demonstration until May 1915 (Glanfield 2001: 14).

The response to Pancho Villa's raid into New Mexico, in March 1916, proved how quickly the Army could mechanize locally if incentivized and authorized. The cavalry brigade was supported logistically by 108 trucks, across four Motor Truck Companies. By June, the Quartermaster Corps purchased 805 automobiles (including 61 motorcycles). All were wheeled. Only 8 were tractors (Drake 1919: 298).

On 6th April 1917, the US Congress declared war on Germany, and authorized an American Expeditionary Force (AEF) that would eventually rival any Western European army in scale and mechanization – and at epic pace. General John J. Pershing received the first report from his Military Mission to France on 21st May. This focused on British and French operations, including with tanks. Pershing immediately despatched several committees to study British and French equipment, structure, and tactics (Wilson 1988: 8). By July, five American divisions were training with the British behind the front lines in northern France.

However, American investigation of tanks was neither quick nor meritorious. Pershing waited more than three months after the declaration of war to appoint a Tank Board (19th July). Within days, it reported on the latest British doctrine, but its first visit to the British Tank Corps HQ waited until 24th August. Only two offficers arrived – late at night, and drunk (Hofmann 1999: 93). Fuller, who led doctrine and requirements for the Tank Corps, was supposed to be their principal helper:

> The next morning the Major showed me a paper he had written on tanks – it was marked "very secret" and "shown to no one." Then he folded it up and put it into his pocket. Some weeks later it was found in an "estimation" at Arras, and as it mentioned tanks it was sent on to us. (Fuller 1936: 157-158)

Pershing's appointments were unmeritorious, with privileges lasting through World War II. He did not involve the Motor Transport Group, even though it had landed in June. In September, he broke up the Tank Board, and ordered two Majors of Ordnance (James A. Drain; H.W. Alden) to confer with the British and French, but Ordnance was focused on artillery. Soon, Field Artillery officers were involved.

To their credit, Drain and Alden reached reasonable requirements: heavy tanks, either British or American; and light tanks, either French or American. Later in September, the French and British agreed an American tank force of equal scale, but could not promise supplies (Wilson 1988: 16-17).

This was the point when Pershing (who was determining requirements in the field with little input from the War Department) should have required American tanks. However, he did not regard tanks as revolutionary. His messages urged the War Department to train "open warfare" and to focus on pedestrian equipment. On 19th October, he added: "Close adherence is urged to the central idea that the essential principles of war have not changed, that the rifle and the bayonet remain the supreme weapons of the infantry soldier and that the ultimate success of the army depends on their proper use in warfare" (Rainey 1983: 34).

Pershing wanted tanks, but would wait on foreign supplies. Worse, he deferred to an unqualified friend. In 1915, 30-year-old Lieutenant George S. Patton had built an unusually close relationship with Pershing, then commanding the 8th Cavalry Regiment at Fort Bliss, Texas, and courting Patton's older sister (after losing his wife and three of his four children to a fire). Patton joined his staff, and became his personal aide in France. Bored with subsequent duties, in November Patton secured command of the American light tank school in France. His interest (he admitted) was promotion, not mechanization. On 10th November, Drain and Alden recommended an American copy of the FT, but Pershing waited on Patton. Patton slowly took advice from Renault and a friend in the Field Artillery, before, on 12th December, completing a prescription for using FT tanks like cavalry, for "pursuit" operations, principally because he imagined the type closest to a horse (Wilson 1999: 3-4; Wright 2000: 192; Eisenhower 2012: 29).

The FT was the best light tank of the war, but his choice stopped the US turning

Patton with a FT, armed with a 37-mm gun, circa June 1918.

The Holt "gas-electric tank" in 1918.

its superior automotive industry to the design of revolutionary tanks. Moreover, neither Pershing or Patton moved with sufficient urgency to get the American copy (M1917) into the field before the war ended. Pershing appointed the US Army Tank Service's commander (Brigadier-General Samuel Rockenbach) on 22nd December, effective 26th January. Rockenbach was meritorious, but never controlled acquisitions. Patton did not send his second-in-command (Elgin Braine) home with Renault's plans until 22nd February.

Patton received the first draft of tank officers from the US on 8th January, the first ten FTs on 27th March. In June, the French promised enough FTs for two light battalions, although they sent only 15 that month. The British promised enough Mark V Heavy Tanks for the 1st Tank Battalion (later: 301st Heavy), which joined the Tank Training Center at Bovington on 9th April. By 20th August, the Tank Service had 1,200 trained men in France, 1,200 men training in England, and the personnel of 12 light tank companies enroute from the US to France. Yet tanks were only just arriving for three units (Greenhalgh 2000: 824-825; Johnson 2003: 35).

By August 1918, Patton had rocketed from Captain to Lieutenant-Colonel, in command of the 1st and only Tank Brigade. On 12th September, its two battalions joined the first attack in France by a US field army. The 301st Heavy Tank Battalion arrived from Britain that month (as part of a British tank brigade), and became the first American heavy tank unit to fight (29th September). The light battalions lost more tanks than they received, so were consolidated as a company in late October.

The M1917 arrived after the armistice – 19 months after the US declared war. US authorities came up with ridiculous excuses: conversion of measures from metric to imperial; difficulties sourcing armor plate; management of more than 20 contractors, and more subcontractors (Wilson 1988: 91). The Army had looked forward to British Mark VI tanks, until the British cancelled it. Ordnance cooperated in developing the Mark VIII tank, but American production did not start until 1919.

Meanwhile, largely private entrepreneurs developed regrettable offerings. Holt stretched the Holt 75's running gear and added a 90-hp engine, an electric transmission, an armored superstructure, a 75-mm mountain gun in the front, and

The Russian tricycle in August 1915.

a machine-gun in each side. As with all Holts, its mobility was insufficient for a battlefield. Other offerings included a steam tank, a "skeleton tank" (named after its external frame), and two unambitious light tanks by Ford (described in the next chapter). American automotive capacities had been wasted, for which the root cause was lack of realistic urgency and specifications from the field (see Table 3).

Russia

Russia did not produce any tanks during the First World War. It produced two vehicles that are often asserted as the first tanks, even though one was wheeled, and the other was neither armed nor armored.

The *Vezdekhod* (meaning: all-terrain vehicle) was a small unarmored car, with a single rubberized fabric track rolling around drums. Steering was effected by a wheel to each side, controlled mechanically from inside the vehicle. At trials in March 1915, it reached 25 kmh (17 mph), but it was never armored or armed.

In August 1915, the Imperial Russian Army tried a large tricycle (inaccurately known as the "Tsar Tank") with two front wheels (27 feet or 8.2 meters in diameter) and a smaller rear wheel (5 feet or 1.5 meters). It became stuck and was abandoned. The Bolsheviks scrapped it in 1923. Armaments and armor were never completed (Ford 2011: 226-227).

Imperial Russia faced a long mobile front from the Baltic to the Caucasus, so its requirement for mechanization was high. However, its economy was largely agricultural. It relied on imported vehicles, including British armored cars. Tanks would have been most useful if the few cities were ever fortified. Even then, heavy weapons were difficult to concentrate given the poor communications. In 1917, the regime collapsed and reached an armistice with the Central Powers. Tsarist "White Russian" forces used British armored cars and French FT tanks against the Bolsheviks in 1918, and British heavy and medium tanks in 1919, some with British crews (Fuller 1936: 374; Kenez 1977: 22, 323; Fletcher 2001: 173).

Italy

Italy did not join the war until May 1915. Given a mountainous border with Austro-Hungary, the requirement for fighting vehicles was low. The stagnation of the front, and British revelation of the tank in September 1916, prompted (in the next month) engagement of Fiat to develop an equivalent (eventually known as Fiat 2000). Evaluation of a Schneider tank, locally, in the Spring, confirmed preferences for something heavy. In June 1917, Fiat demonstrated a chassis, although it did not complete the tank or a second, similar pilot until February 1918. Each was closer in size, weight, armament, and armor to the A7V, with a specified weight of 40 tons (39 long; 44 US), a 65-mm gun in a turret, and seven machine-guns around the hull.

By November 1918, the Italian Army counted seven FT tanks, two Fiat 2000 heavy tanks, and one Schneider heavy tank in service. In December, the infantry arm in Turin formed its first armored unit (*1a Batteria Autonoma Carri d'Assalto*; 1st Independent Battery, Assault Tanks), with the second Fiat 2000 and three French FT light tanks. In 1919, it transferred to Libya to counter insurgents there (Cappellano and Battistelli 2012: 10-11).

Meanwhile, Fiat developed an Italian version of the FT, with a more powerful engine and twin 6.5mm machine-guns. Delivery was scheduled for May 1919, but (given the end of the war) was not piloted until August 1920. Late in 1921, it was accepted into service as the "Fiat 3000 Model 1921 Assault Tank" (*Carro d'assalto Fiat 3000 Modello 1921*) (Cappellano and Battistelli 2012: 4-5).

Given a change in the operational situation, and Allied inspiration, Italy had creditably turned its innovative automotive sector to the development of tanks to compete with the best of the period (see Table 5).

The second pilot Fiat 2000, circa February 1918

The Dominions

Britain was joined at war immediately by its four Dominions: Canada, South Africa, Australia, and New Zealand. Their forces proved interested and competent in mechanized warfare. However, some were focused outside of France, with little requirement for tanks. All were largely dependent on Britain for heavy armaments.

South African ground forces fought in Africa and the Middle East, with only one infantry brigade in France, and no plan to add tank units.

Australian and New Zealand forces fought the Ottoman Empire, until 1916, when most transferred to France. The Australians, with three divisions in France, had the greater operational requirement for tanks, but their government never authorized any. The New Zealanders had one division there: in 1918, their government programmed a tank battalion, but their Army HQ obstructed. The main barrier to new arms, for all the Allies, including Britain, was the overall shortage of soldiers, given high consumption in the senior arms.

Of Dominion forces, only Canada's was always focused in France. On the 15th of September, 1914, a retired French officer in Canada (Major Raymond Brutinel), with the financial support of a consortium led by Sir Clifford Sifton, designated 1st Automobile Machine-Gun Brigade. This landed in England from October to February. On 16th May, it was re-designated 1st Canadian Motor Machine-Gun Brigade. It arrived in France in June 1915 and fought through the end of the war. Thus, the Canadian Army was ready with an equivalent to the same arm that the British Army would turn into the first user of tanks. Unfortunately, British supply of tanks remained uncertain through 1917. Canada raised its 1st Tank Battalion in March 1918. In June, the personnel enshipped for Britain, although they did not transfer to the Tank Training Centre for final training until August. Their training remained incomplete at the end of the war. Three more battalions had been programmed but not raised (Fuller 1920, pp. 64-67, 163).

Conclusion

As Table 4 shows, only Britain, France, German, and Italy deployed tanks of their own design during World War I. Another four countries (America, Canada, New Zealand, and White Russia) used foreign tanks before the end of the war, of which two (Canada and New Zealand) used them for only training.

America would have deployed tanks of its own design during the Spring 1919 offensive. Canada would have deployed at least one unit then, and New Zealand would have deployed only one, in both cases with British tanks.

An offensive posture, a sedentary front, and either foreign supplies or a heavy automotive sector were necessary, but none was sufficient. The British wasted about a year on projects disconnected from field requirements. The French were late to put the correct requirement and supplier together. The US Army neglected and misdirected its home industry. The Italians had a much weaker requirement and industry than America, but still got a turreted heavy tank into service in 1918.

The Russians were weaker still in industrial capacity and communications, faced a more extensive front, and collapsed into civil war, so their first tanks were French and British. Canada and New Zealand efficiently waited on British tanks, although at cost in time of deploying their own units.

The timing of tanks is different to the qualities of tanks, which are the subjects of the next chapter.

Country	Side	Democratic-ness (0-20 scale)	Military expenditure, 1914-1918 (US$)	Industrial capabilities, average year, 1914-1918 (% of all states)	First operational use of tanks	Tanks of own design acquired by armistice	Peak trained tank personnel	Peak tank units	Types piloted 1916-1919	Average effectiveness, efficiency
Britain	Western Allies	18	28,248,359	14.68	September 1916	2,619	13,336	22 organized, of which 18 fought	26	0.33, 0.41
France	Western Allies	18	22,897,000	8.24	April 1917	5,300	14,649	26	5	0.33, 0.42
Germany	Central Powers	12	27,702,000	15.80	March 1918 (December 1917 with British tanks)	20 (30 open carrier variants and >50 British)	4,000	1	6	0.35, 0.38
USA	Western Allies	20	8,461,084	24.01	September 1918 (with British and French tanks)	79 (514 French and 46 British)	14,000	9 organized, of which 3 fought	8	0.31, 0.39
Russia	Allies until 1917; then factions on both sides	4 (9 for revolutionary regime)	14,022,741	10.68	1918 (White Russians)	0 (some French tanks)	500	1	0	-
Italy	Western Allies from 1915	9	783,886	3.19	1918 at home 1919 in Libya	2	500	1	1	0.30, 0.36
Canada	Western Allies	19	?	1.01	-	0 (British tanks used in training)	500	1 raised, another 3 programmed	0	-
New Zealand	Western Allies	20	?	0.10	-	0 (British tanks used in training)	500	1 programmed	0	-
Australia	Western Allies	20	?	0.69	-	0	0	1 considered	0	-
Austro-Hungary	Central Powers	6	10,495,000	4.92	-	0	0	0	0	-
Turkey	Central Powers	9	224,127	1.01	-	0	0	0	0	-

Table 4: Tank acquisitions, economics, and politics of the eleven great powers of the First World War, ordered by first operational use and peak tank units. Additional sources: Correlates of War dataset (for military and economic data); Polity V dataset (for democraticness).

Notes: tank pilots, effectiveness, and efficiency (see Appendix for methodology) are calculated for years from 1916 to 1919 inclusive; economic data for Canada, New Zealand, and Australia are for year 1920, when their entries begin in the datasets.

197..   *Engl. Panzerauto (Tank)*

This Mark II Male was captured on 11th April 1917, near Arras

This Mark III, in training in 1917, reveals the length of the six-pounder used in the first three Marks.

A Mark IV, with the shorter six-pounder, is tried with the first Tadpole, in France, March 1918.

CHAPTER 3

Why Western tanks were best

Britain, France, Germany, Italy, and America (in order) were the only countries to develop tanks by the end of 1918. In this chapter, I compare the qualities of their designs, including designs that never deployed. Britain developed the most types, so the first sections focus on Britain, starting with its many heavy tanks (compared by mobility, lethality, and survivability).

British Heavy Tanks: Mobility

The abilities of British heavies to cross trenches, steps, craters, and mud were unmatched by foreign peers, although most of the latter were faster and easier to carry (see Table 5). Even the Mark I out-performed most foreign tanks in these regards, for many years. This explains why the British hardly respecified mobility between the first four marks.

The only modification to the Mark I's mobility was to abandon the steering tail, as not worth the trouble. The Mark II (first used 9th April 1917) was designed with a narrower driver's tower so that wider tracks could be fitted if required, although these were resented for their additional resistance to steering (Fletcher 2001: 38). For the Mark III, the vision slits in front of the driver were rearranged. Since most Mark IIIs stayed in Britain, most were never armed (Glanfield 2001: 279; Fletcher 2004: 42-43). The Mark IV (first used 7th June 1917) featured retractable sponsons (rather than the detachable sponsons of previous marks) and a new fuel system. Mark IV Males mounted shorter 6-pounder guns, because the longer gun had dug into the ground when the tank pitched (Glanfield 2001: 280; Fletcher 2001: 69).

As the Germans widened their trenches, and British operations became more ambitious, most subsequent improvements were in mobility. An extended tail ("Tadpole") was developed for the Mark IV in March 1918, but this reduced agility, power-to-weight, and reliability, so, although 300 Tadpoles were delivered, none was used in combat.

The Mark V (first used 4th July 1918) was no longer than the Mark IV, but introduced an epicyclic gearbox, so that steering could be controlled by one man. Previous marks had required four men: the nominal "driver" operated the wheeled tail; gears-men controlled the geared speed to each track; and the commander operated the brakes on each track. The commander had previously been positioned at the front beside the driver. In the Mark V, he was given a tower towards the rear, with loopholes in the sides, in place of the flush circular hatch. A hinged top hatch could be used for escape, or to access an unditching beam that could be slid forward along rails (if fitted) for attachment to the tracks.

The last wartime design to see action (8th August 1918) was the Mark V* (Mark Five Star), a longer version of Mark V – and thus more difficult to steer, heavier, and less reliable. The Mark V** (Five Star Star) was the same length, but easier to steer thanks to reduced track-ground contact and rearward-mounted engine (thereby shifting the center of gravity). The driver's and commander's towers were consolidated as one larger compartment. An uprated engine improved mobility

This Mark V Male shows the new command tower behind the driver's tower.

A Female Mark V* on trial at Dollis Hill in 1918.

The Mark VI mock-up of February 1917.

This is the first British Mark VIII, delivered in October 1918.

and reliability (Fletcher 2001: 140-142; 161-162).

The Mark VI was a radical competitor to the Mark V, although the Mark V was ready quick enough that the Mark VI did not proceed beyond a mock-up (delivered 22nd February 1917). The Mark VI would have featured: epicyclic steering, like the Mark V; wider tracks (29 inches; 0.75 m), for better ground flotation; and shorter length, for improved steerability (although with inferior obstacle-crossing).

The Mark VII was piloted in July 1918 with a hydraulic transmission that proved too bulky and difficult to cool. The Mark IX (June 1918) was primarily a carrier, but designated a tank given an initial specification for convertibility to sponsons. It was delivered with two machine-gun mountings (front and rear respectively).

The Mark VIII was a British design, although two US Army officers promoted American interests, of whom one patented a male sponson for this tank (pivoting into the tank, rather than sliding on rails). The Mark VIII was a revolutionary break from the previous series, although the shape was similar. The Mark VIII was the most mobile off road, thanks to a longer hull (about 2 feet or 0.6 m longer than a Mark V**), wider tracks, and more power. The caveat is that the Mark VIII was more difficult to steer: the tracks were wider and longer, and the hull was 12 inches (0.3 m) narrower than any previous Male tank.

The engine was a V12, in contrast to Britain's previous in-line six cylinder tank engines. The British commissioned their normal supplier (Harry Ricardo), but the Americans chose an aero-engine ("Liberty"), which was slightly less powerful and much less reliable, given allocation of cheap materials and inadequate ruggedizing. In any case, prioritization of aero-engines delayed the tank engine's delivery. The international assembly program (in France) was delayed by mal-coordination and under-resourcing, so no components were ever sent to France. One Mark VIII was piloted in Britain in October (Greenhalgh 2000: 828-835; Fletcher 2001: 165-167).

A longer version (Mark VIII*) was drawn but not developed.

British Heavy Tanks: Lethality

Increasing length, in pursuit of wider trench crossing, drove up weight, which was the main reason why the British barely improved survivability, and did not improve lethality (except in fighting and command arrangements) during the war.

The largest gun ever deployed in a British tank of World War I was the 57-mm six-pounder, which was smaller in caliber than the 75-mm guns in French heavy tanks and German super-heavy designs. The six-pounder in Marks I, II, and III was larger in capacity than the A7V's 57-mm gun, but the shorter six-pounder was not.

The sponsons allowed for wider distribution of fire than the forward mountings on French and German heavy tanks, although less efficiently than the revolving turret of the French light and Italian heavy tanks.[1]

Males mounted one 57-mm six-pounder gun and one machine-gun on each side, while females mounted two machine-guns on each side. The six-pounder fired high-explosive shells of more use against targets behind cover, but machine-guns could be stowed with more ammunition. Additionally, they were supposed to be dismounted and carried forward when the tank inevitably bogged down, broke down, ran up against an impassable obstacle, or ran out of fuel.[2]

Machine-guns also offered much higher muzzle velocity than the larger caliber guns mounted in tanks during this period. Muzzle velocity suggests accuracy. Larger caliber guns could fire to longer ranges, at higher parabolic trajectories, but in this era tanks were firing directly at close ranges, too close to see any falling trajectory in machine-gun bullets.

A hermaphrodite Mark V (a 57-mm gun on one side, two machine-guns on the other) was ordered in July 1918, after realization that Females would be outgunned by A7Vs. (In the first tank on tank fight, on 24th April, an A7V had driven off two Mark IV Females, before being driven off by a Male.) Most Mark Vs were converted by the end of the war. However, they suffered inferior mobility and reliability due to lack of balance. They predominated during the occupation of Germany, where their asymmetry did not affect mobility on hard roads. They also predominated during intervention in southern Russia in Summer 1919, when the ground was hard (Fletcher 2001: 142, 159, 173-175).

Female versions were given up for the Mark VIII. The British chose for their version (named "International") seven machine-guns. The Americans deleted the two in the side doors, and added a "deflector plate" so that fire from the command tower would reach the hidden area behind the tail of their version ("Liberty").

The Mark VI did not proceed beyond mock-up, so does not get into my dataset, but was unique for being configured like French and German heavies. Compared to Marks I to V, the width from inner to outer frames was increased (from 1'5" to 2'2"; 432 mm to 660 mm). In order to stay within the railway loading envelope, sponsons were abandoned. More internal width allowed the engine be packaged to one side, leaving space in the center for a tall tower ("fighting chamber"), in which the crew could stand upright. This was designed with machine-guns at each corner.

---

1 Each six-pounder swept an arc of 121 degrees. The two lines of fire converged some 60 yards (55 m) in front of the tank. One machine-gun was mounted to the rear of each six-pounder, with a sweep mostly rearwards. Females mounted a machine-gun in each of two mountings in each sponson. These pivoted independently across 120 degrees, together covering 180 degrees (Glanfield 2001: 275; Fletcher 2004: 51).

2 Mark I and Mark II Females carried five water-cooled, belt-fed Vickers medium machine-guns (four in the sponsons, plus a spare) and one air-cooled, strip-fed Hotchkiss (front). The Male carried three Hotchkiss machine-guns (front; left side; right side), plus a spare (Williams-Ellis and Williams-Ellis 1920: 26-27). Most Female Mark IIIs received air-cooled (heat sink and jacket), magazine-fed Lewis guns instead of Vickers guns. All Mark IVs received Lewis guns in place of both Vickers and Hotchkiss guns. From Mark V, Hotchkiss guns were the only machine-guns issued with British heavy and medium tanks. The Mark IV to Mark VII Males are officially listed with four machine-guns, Females with six. One user specified five, with 5,500 rounds, in the Male Marks IV, V, and V* (Lieutenant-Colonel H. Boyd-Rochfort, 3rd Tank Group, "Headings for a lecture to infantry fighting personnel," late 1918, RACTM E1972.267). The Mark V was first to feature a rear mounting for a Hotchkiss. The Mark V* gained mountings in the front and rear of the command tower. The Mark VI and Mark VIII did not have a Female version.

Machine-guns could be mounted in each side door. A 57-mm gun was mounted in the front, with traverse of 45 degrees (limited by projecting "horns" carrying the tracks).

British Heavy Tanks: Survivability

From April 1915, Landships were specified with 12-mm armor, as proof against the reversed lead-cored bullets the Germans were firing against infantry shields. German 7.92-mm steel-cored armor-piercing bullets could perforate 12-mm, before the Germans deployed larger caliber rifles that could perforate any British tank of the war.

The fronts of Marks I to IV were 12-mm thick, but the sides were 8-mm thick. The Mark II and Mark III tanks were ordered as training vehicles with soft steel, which was not proof against small-arms fire except at unusual ranges or angles of attack. (Too few Mark Is had been ordered in the first place; and Mark IVs were not delivered until March 1917.) Some Mark IIs, at least, were used in combat. Armor plates were acquired for bolting to the sides and (as spaced armor) to the roof, but never fitted. Some Females were armed with hardened-steel gun sponsons taken from Mark I tanks (Glanfield 2001: 278; Fletcher 2004: 38-40).

The right-hand sponson on a Female Mark V** at the RACTM.

The Mark III was the first to be designed with 12-mm plates on the sides as well as the front. On the Mark V (and Medium A), front thickness increased to 14 mm, on the Mark VIII to 16 mm. The Mark VIII's front was the narrowest, but taller.

For the Mark IV, the fuel tank was relocated from inside the upper front interior to outside the lower rear, and was assembled with armored plates. (The earlier fuel system was fed by gravity, while the latter included an electric pump.)

For Marks I, II, and III, the exhaust was located on top, where it was easily seen emitting sparks and flame. The Mark IV's exhaust was relocated to the rear, and fitted with a silencer, which dampened noise and sparks.

The side escape doors proved satisfactory on Mark I Males, but were smaller on Females, to fit below the machine-gun mountings. Moreover, whereas the Male door was rear-facing, the Female door was located on the side, which left it more exposed to fire from the front. A larger Female door was standardized early in the production of Mark IIIs, given a smaller sponson (with Lewis gun mountings).

British Medium Tanks

The British were unique in the First World War for issuing medium tanks (14-20 long tons; 15-22 US tons). These boasted the same armor as most British Heavies, practically the same lethality as Female Heavies, and better speed. Male Mediums were planned but interrupted by the end of the war.

The Medium A ("Whippet"), which was first used in March 1918, proved its requirement for exploiting breaches punched by the heavies. The Medium B and Medium C were produced by the end of the war but not deployed. They were

This Medium A is viewed from its left front. The tower was designed with a machine-gun mounting in four sides, and a driver's position at its right front.

stop-gaps, pending the Medium D, which was intended for use in Spring 1919, but never fully developed as required in 1918. Each evolution improved speed, range, and reliability, at the expense of lethality and survivability (see Table 5), although peacetime was partly to blame for this trend.

French tanks

The first two French tanks were medium-heavy by British standards. Both utilized lengthened Baby Holt 45 running gear. The second and longer tank – St. Chamond – crossed wider trenches (7'10.5"; 2.4 m) than the Schneider (5'11"; 1.8 m), but less than the first mark of British tank (by 2 feet; 0.6 m). It climbed a step of just 1'4" (0.4 m), half as high as the Schneider, and less than a third as high as the British Mark I. Even the St. Chamond's trench-crossing was somewhat artificial, because its extended superstructure and longer gun were likelier to dig into rolling ground. The Germans quickly widened their trenches to defeat the French tanks.

The Schneider was armed with a short 75-mm gun/howitzer (in a sponson on the right) and two machine-guns (sides), while the Saint-Chamond had a 75-mm field gun (front) and four machine-guns (front, rear, sides). Both were assembled with 11.5-mm plates. To defeat German 7.92-mm AP bullets, in Spring 1917 spaced armor plates were added.

In November 1917, the French started tests of a larger tank (FCM 1A), weighing more than 40 metric tons, with a 105-mm howitzer in a turret, and armor up to 35 mm thick. However, development was under-funded and unhurried, in favor of designs for yet more powerful heavy tanks, all of which were relegated behind an Allied agreement to share a single heavy type (Britain's Mark VIII).

The FT light tank could climb in and out of wide gaps that might defeat the French heavies, thanks to a high, large, forward drive wheel, a rounded tail, and provision for the engine to receive fuel and air at high inclines. The turret was armed first with a machine-gun, which was sufficient for its initial requirement to support infantry against enemy infantry. A second version (1918) was armed with a 37-mm gun, whose shells were more effective than bullets against fortifications. However, its great inferiority in muzzle velocity is enough to make the second version compute as inferior in effectiveness overall (see Graph 1). In both cases, the crew remained two men. Thus, one FT represented one-quarter the burden of a British heavy tank in personnel, size, and weight (see Table 5).

Nevertheless, the British Tank Corps preferred its heavy and medium tanks. On 17th January 1918, JFC Fuller (operations chief) and F. Elliot Hotblack (intelligence chief) were shown equipment by their French equivalents at Compiègne.

> I found their heavy tank a kind of kitchen-range on tracks – unblushingly useless, and their small Renault machines were nothing more than cleverly made mountings for battalion machine-guns. The General [Estienne] did not impress me, though I found him to be an amusing little dud. The whole atmosphere of these Headquarters was both refreshing and depressing; it was nothing but cannon and women and women and cannon. Apparently everyone wanted to fill his tank with seventy-fives and his billet with chorus girls. (Fuller 1936: 232)

In May 1918, the French Minister of Armaments (Louis Loucheur) suggested an exchange of 500 FTs for 100 British Mark V heavy tanks. The War Office accepted 10 FT17s for trials in France. In June, the French promised to exchange 1,500 FTs for 900 Mark VIII Heavies, but neither the extra 1,500 FTs nor any Mark VIII heavy tanks arrived before peacetime (Greenhalgh 2000: 829-830).

Most French tanks serving in the final months of the First World War and between the world wars were FTs. It was the most exported and copied tank of the period, and was still in frontline French and foreign service in 1940.

German tanks

The Germans relied on captured British Mark IV tanks for their initial tank operation in December 1917. In time, the Germans took captured British Medium A tanks and French FT17 light tanks into service too.

The first wholly German design to be used (March 1918) was the A7V. This was the tallest and widest tank to see action in the Great War, and almost the heaviest (the Mark V* was slightly heavier). Compared to the St. Chamond, it offered a shorter hull, longer ground contact, more ground pressure (given more weight), less stability, lower ground clearance (16"; 0.4 m), and inferior trench-crossing (6 feet: 1.8 m). On the other hand, it was the fastest (10 mph; 16 km), best armed, and thickest armored (30 mm). A 57-mm gun was mounted in the front with limited traverse; two machine guns were mounted each side, two in the rear. Exceptionally, armor covered most of the running gear. Fuller gives a fair summary:

> The chief characteristics of this tank were: its good speed on smooth ground, on which it could attain some 8 miles an hour; its inability to cross almost any type of trench or shelled ground on account of its shape. In weight it was about 40 tons, it carried very thick armor[,] especially in front, capable of withstanding AP bullets at close range and field gun shells, not firing AP ammunition, at long. It was, however, very vulnerable to the splash of ordinary bullets on account of the crevices and joints in its armor. The most interesting feature of this otherwise indifferent machine was that its tracks were provided with spring bogies [developed by Joseph Vollmer]. The use of sprung tracks in so heavy a tank was the only progressive step shown in the German effort at tank production. (Fuller 1920: 212-213)

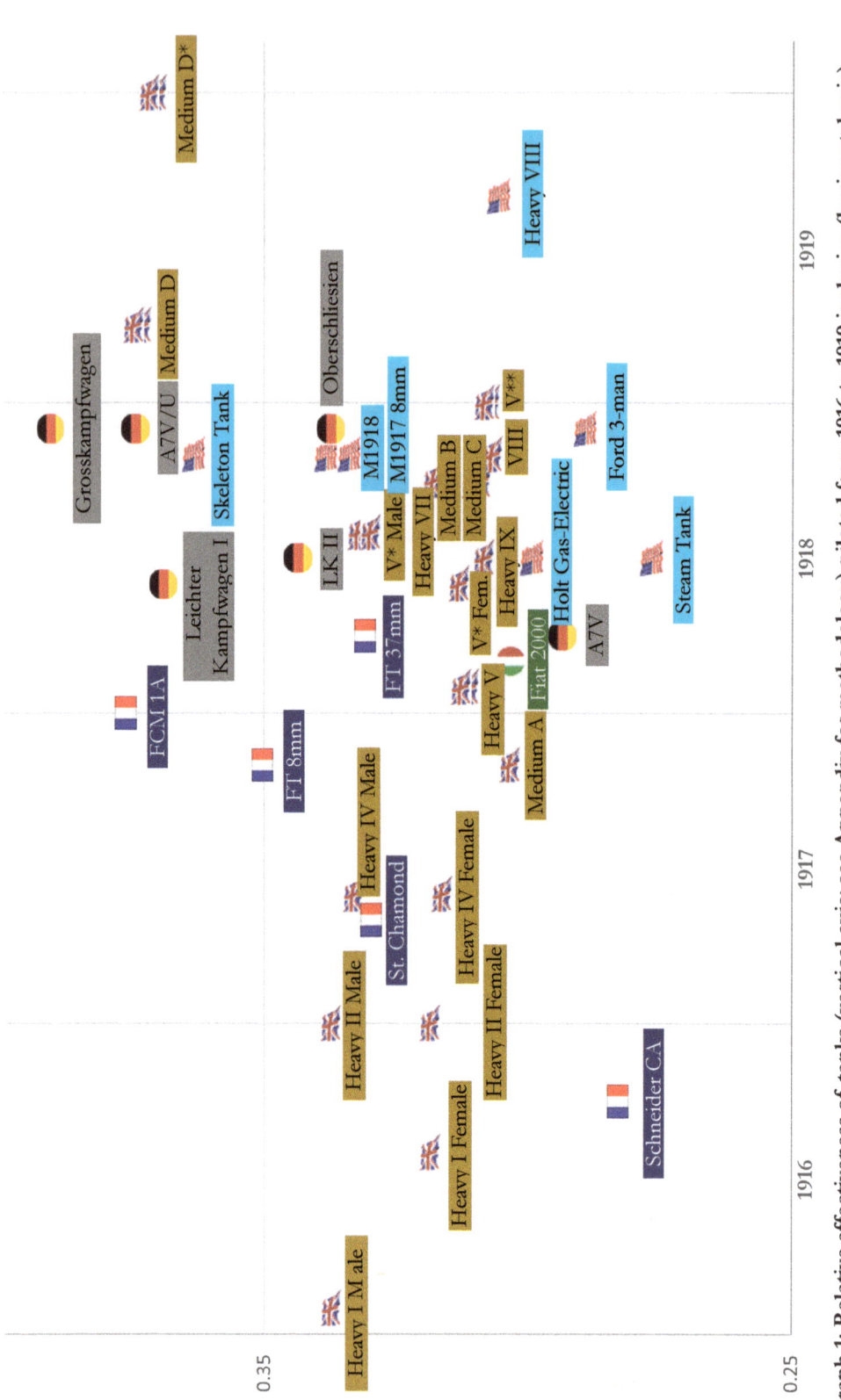

Graph 1: Relative effectiveness of tanks (vertical axis; see Appendix for methodology) piloted from 1916 to 1919 inclusive (horizontal axis).

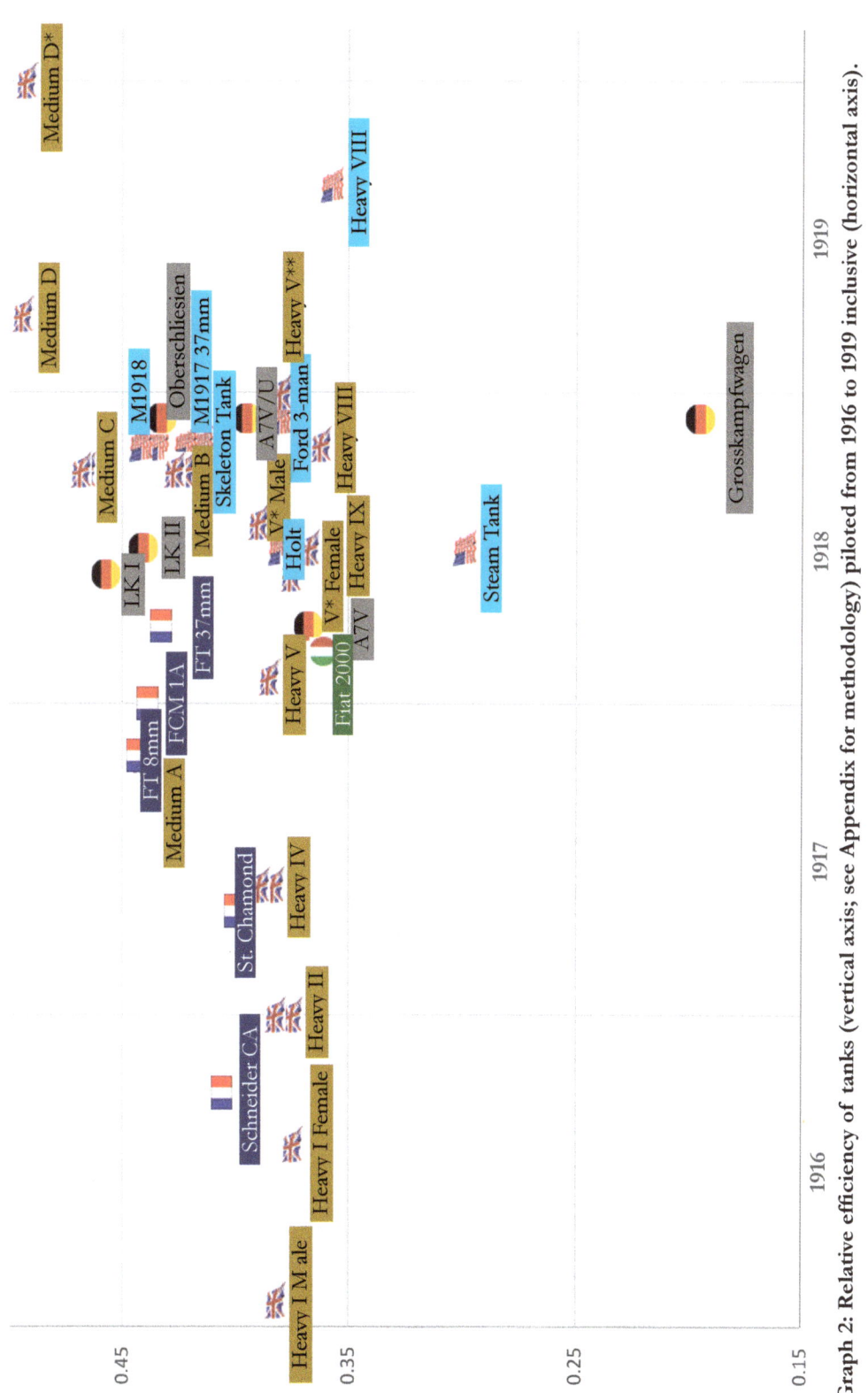

Graph 2: Relative efficiency of tanks (vertical axis; see Appendix for methodology) piloted from 1916 to 1919 inclusive (horizontal axis).

Fuller admitted that the British were just as shocked by A7Vs on 21st March 1918 as the Germans by Mark Is on 15th September 1916, and more shocked by an attack on 8th October 1918. He cited a captured document (now lost) that had been issued by German XVII Corps at some point during those months: "Our own tanks strengthen the morale of the infantry to a tremendous extent, even if employed only in small numbers, and experience has shown that they have a considerable demoralizing effect on the hostile infantry." (Fuller 1920: 214-215)

The A7Vs were reserved for hard flat terrain, while the Germans developed a copy of the British Mark IV Male for assaulting trenches. Hence the designation A7V/U, where the "U" is short for *Unlaufende Ketten* (meaning: all-around tracks). The A7V's suspended running gear was carried forward, in pursuit of more speed. One pilot was built from September to November 1918, too late to see action.

A copy of the Medium A was designated a light tank (*Leichter Kampfwagen*), given faster speed and easier driving. Track units were mounted externally on a Daimler car's axles. A rotating turret carried one machine-gun and a third crewman (relieving the commander of operating the armament). This was piloted in May 1918, a month before a larger version (*LK II*), which would have mounted a 37-mm or 57-mm gun. (As with the FTs, the LK II's effectiveness score, even with 57-mm gun, computes lower than for LK I, due to much lower muzzle velocity and a slight decline in mobility: see Graph 1.) Mass production was not delivered before the armistice. The soundness of the design is indicated by Swedish use, from 1921 to 1938, with local engines and machine-guns, as *Stridsvagn M21*.

The Germans designed a medium tank that would have outmatched any tank deployed, if finished in time. Its classification (*Sturmpanzerwagen*; assault armored vehicle) indicates the ambition: an assault tank, as well armed and armored as British heavy tanks, but lighter, smaller, and faster. The smaller size meant shorter trench-crossing capability, but its ability to traverse uneven ground was superior to the A7V's, given longer ground contact and taller forward profile. A fully rotating turret mounted the same gun as in the front of the A7V. The *Oberschlesien Eisenwerk* (Upper Silesian Ironworks) almost completed two pilots when the war ended.

The designer of the A7V, A7V/U, and LK I (Joseph Vollmer) designed also a very large tank (*Grosskampfwagen*; K-Wagen), with multiple 77-mm guns, and armor as thick as the A7V's, but with such powerful engines that its power-weight ratio was superior. Two pilots were almost complete at the end of the war, but would be dismantled under Allied supervision, without tests or trials.

The A7V/U at the end of the war.

(Above) Leichter Kampfwagen I
(Middle) Stridsvagn M21
(Bottom) Grosskampfwagen

M1918, M1917, and Liberty tanks on display in 1920.

Italian tanks

The Fiat 2000 was closest in specifications to the German A7V: weight of 40 metric tons, a 65-mm gun in a turret, seven machine-guns in the hull (one on each corner, one in each side, and one at the front), and 20-mm armor plates. It was more mobile than French and German heavy tanks, given longer and taller running gear, sprung bogies, and superior transmission, but did not match the obstacle-crossing of the British heavy tanks (Cappellano and Battistelli, 2012: 4-5).

American tanks

The Americans did not deploy their own designs before the end of the war. In any case, those designs are best characterized as unambitious or parochial.

The first design to be standardized (Six-Ton Tank Model 1917; M1917) was a copy of the FT, without improving on the French design. Most American products were armed with one machine-gun.

In early 1918, the Ordnance Department, without any requirement or approval from the users, contracted with Ford Motor Company on promise of lower cost, quicker production, and better mechanical reliability. Ford designed a turret-less tracked vehicle, with space for a machine-gunner and a driver, side-by-side, behind 13-mm armor. Its exceptionalisms were lowest height (a factor in survivability) and highest power-to-weight ratio yet for a tank, although it was not quite as fast or as effective in crossing obstacles as the other light tanks. It scores well for effectiveness (see Graph 1) and efficiency (Graph 2) overall, but these indices do not capture complaints about its cramped interior, poor vision, and rough ride. Although the Army standardized it as a tank (Three-Ton M1918), the Tank Service approved it as a light artillery tractor or an emergency substitute for FT and M1917. In any case, Ford never made good on its promise for quick production. Although 15,000 had been ordered, only 15 were delivered before the armistice, when the contract was canceled. A few were sent to France for testing by tankers, who found it unsuited for the battlefield (Wilson 1988: 94-96; Wilson 1999: 9-11; Cameron 2008: 7).

Ford developed a three-man version, with a turret, but without improving on the FT. Holt's Gas-Electric tank was equivalent to the Schneider tank, and thus redundant.

The only American pilot of similar size to a British heavy weighed one-third as much. The "Skeleton"/"Spider" tank aimed for similar trench-crossing, but lighter weight by running the tracks around a frame external to an armored compartment (for two men, two engines, and a machine-gun) (see Table 5). This was delivered too late and too privately (by Pioneer Tractor Company) to hold official attention.

Date of pilot	Type	Country	Max. gun caliber (mm)	Barrel length (mm)	Gun capacity (mm³)	Muzzle velocity (m/s)	Max. armor (mm)	Height (m)	Weight (metric tons)	Nominal ground pressure (kN/M2)	Engine power to weight (bhp/ton)	Speed (km/hr)	Operating range (km)	Step (m)
1916-01	Heavy 1, Male	British	57	2280	5,818,010	560	12	2.45	28.4	87	3.7	6	38	1.4
1916-07	Heavy 1, Female	British	7.7	720	33,528	744	12	2.45	27.4	87	3.8	6	38	1.4
1916-09	Schneider CA	French	75	712.5	3,147,729	200	11.5	2.30	13.5	77	4.4	8	80	0.7
1916-12	Heavy 2, Female	British	7.7	720	33,528	744	12	2.45	28.4	87	3.8	6	38	1.4
1916-12	Heavy 2, Male	British	57	2280	5,818,010	560	12	2.45	28.4	87	3.7	6	38	1.4
1916-12	Heavy 3, Female	British	7.7	720	33,528	744	12	2.45	27.4	87	3.8	6	38	1.4
1916-12	Heavy 3, Male	British	57	2280	5,818,010	560	12	2.45	28.4	87	3.7	6	38	1.4
1917-04	Saint-Chamond	French	75	2700	11,928,235	550	11.5	2.35	23.0	78	3.9	12	60	0.4
1917-05	Heavy 4, Female	British	7.7	670	29,760	740	12	2.49	27.4	87	3.8	6	56	1.4
1917-05	Heavy 4, Male	British	57	1311	3,345,356	560	12	2.49	28.4	87	3.7	6	56	1.4
1917-10	Renault FT with MG	French	8	784	39,408	724	22	2.14	6.5	48	6.0	8	60	0.9
1917-12	FCM 1A	French	105	2100	18,183,931	240	35	3	41.4	59	6.0	10	160	1
1917-10	Medium A or Whippet	British	7.7	770	35,856	720	14	2.74	14.2	64	6.3	13	129	0.8
1918-01	Heavy 5 Female	British	7.7	770	35,856	720	14	2.65	29.5	99	5.1	7	72	1.4
1918-01	Heavy 5 Male	British	57	1311	3,345,356	411	14	2.65	29.5	99	5.1	7	72	1.4
1918-02	Fiat 2000	Italian	65	1105	3,666,730	345	20	3.90	40.0		6.0	7	75	1
1918-03	A7V	German	57	1499	3,825,341	401	30	3.30	33.0	112	6.5	16	70	0.7
1918-03	Renault FT, howitzer	French	37	777	835,438	388	22	2.14	6.7	48	5.8	8	60	0.9
1918-05	Heavy 5* Female	British	7.7	770	35,856	720	14	2.65	32.5	92	4.6	7	64	1.4
1918-05	Leichter Kampfwagen	German	7.9	721	35,506	900	14	2.50	6.9		8.7	18	70	0.7
1918-02	Heavy 9	British	7.7	770	35,856	720	10	2.65	27.0	87	5.6	7	32	1.4
1918-06	Leichter Kampfwagen II	German	57	1499	3,825,341	401	14	2.50	8.75		6.9	18	70	0.7
1918-06	Holt Gas-Electric	US	75	800	3,534,292	280	16	2.37	22.7		4.0	10	50	
1918-06	Steam Tank	US	7.6	707	32,073	750	13	3.20	45.0		11.1	6		
1918-07	Heavy 5* Male	British	57	1311	3,345,356	560	14	2.65	33.5	92	4.5	7	64	1.4
1918-07	Heavy 7	British	57	1311	3,345,356	560	14	2.62	33.5	99	4.5	7	80	1.4
1918-09	Medium B Female	British	7.7	770	35,856	720	14	2.56	18.3	76	5.5	10	105	1
1918-09	Medium B Male (design only)	British	40	1560	1,960,354	585	14	2.56	18.3	76	5.5	10	105	1
1918-09	Medium C Female	British	7.7	770	35,856	720	12	3.04	19.8	48	7.6	13	193	1.1
1918-09	Medium C Male (design only)	British	57	2280	5,818,010	411	12	3.04	19.8	48	7.6	13	193	1.1
1918-10	Skeleton or Spider	US	7.6	707	32,064	750	13	2.90	8.2		12.2	9	64	1.4
1918-10	M1917 with MG	US	7.6	707	32,064	750	15	2.29	6.6	48	6.3	9	60	0.9
1918-10	M1917 with howitzer	US	37	740	795,655	367	15	2.29	6.6	48	6.3	9	60	0.9

[continued overleaf]

Date of pilot	Type	Country	Max. gun caliber (mm)	Barrel length (mm)	Gun capacity (mm³)	Muzzle velocity (m/s)	Max. armor (mm)	Height (m)	Weight (metric tons)	Nominal ground pressure (kN/M2)	Engine power to weight (bhp/ton)	Speed (km/hr)	Operating range (km)	Step (m)
1918-10	Ford Two-Man; M1918	US	7.6	707	32,064	750	13	1.80	2.8	78	12.9	13	55	0.5
1918-10	Heavy 8, International	British	57	1311	3,345,356	411	16	3.14	37.6	95	8.0	8	64	1.4
1918-06	Ford Three-Man	US	37	740	795,655	367	13	2.40	6.8		8.8	14.5	70	1.4
1918-11	A7V/U	German	57	1499	3,825,341	401	30	3.14	39.6		5.1	12.5		0.8
1918-11	Sturmpanzerwagen Oberschlesien	German	57	1499	3,825,341	401	14	2.90	19.0		10.0	16	100	0.8
1918-11	Grosskampfwagen	German	77	2079	9,681,125	465	30	2.90	126.0		10.3	8		
1918-12	Heavy V** Female	British	7.7	770	35,856	720	14	2.74	34.5	99	6.5	8	89	1.3
1918-12	Heavy V** Male	British	57	1311	3,345,356	411	14	2.74	35.6	99	6.3	8	89	1.3
1919-03	Medium D Female	British	7.7	770	35,856	720	10	2.81	13.7	83	18.2	47	161	1.2
1919-03	Medium D Male (specified only)	British	57	1311	3,345,356	411	10	2.81	13.7	83	18.2	47	161	1.2
1919-08	Heavy 8, Liberty	US	57	1311	3,345,356	411	16	3.14	39.5	95	7.6	8	64	1.4
1919-12	Medium D* Female	British	7.7	770	35,856	720	10	2.81	13.7	90	18.2	47	161	1.2
1919-12	Medium D* Male (specified only)	British	57	1311	3,345,356	411	10	2.81	13.7	90	18.2	47	161	1.2
1920-02	Medium D** Female	British	7.7	770	35,856	720	10	2.81	13.7	76	18.2	47	161	1.2
1920-02	Medium D** Male (specified only)	British	57	1311	3,345,356	411	10	2.81	13.7	76	18.2	47	161	1.2
1920-08	Fiat 3000 (L5/21)	Italian	37	1480	1,591,311	690	16	2.19	5.5		9.1	21	95	0.6
1921-04	Medium D Modified, Female	British	7.7	770	35,856	720	12	2.81	17.8	75	2.1	29	482	1.2
1921-04	Medium D Modified, Male (specified only)	British	57	1311	3,345,356	411	12	2.81	17.8	75	2.1	29	482	1.2
1921-06	Char 2C or FCM2C	French	75	2700	11,928,235	550	30	4.05	69		5.8	12	150	1.7

Table 5: Specifications and performance of tanks whose platform design started during the First World War (pilots or mass products only). Note: German tanks listed as piloted in November 1918 were days to weeks short of completion at the time of the armistice.

CHAPTER 4

Britain's rise and fall, 1919-1939

After the First World War, Britain remained most innovative, so this chapter starts with Britain. Subsequent chapters consider Britain's former Allies (France, USA, Italy, and Japan), before the USSR, Germany, and Czechoslovakia.

Rise

For Britain, the 1920s was a decade of inventiveness and optimism, despite post-war debts and sorrows. Britain's advantages were many, including Europe's largest industries for automobiles, aviation, shipping, and armaments. The rigors of war had left the Army much more meritorious than in peacetime.

JFC Fuller, then in charge of the General Staff's department for preparing and training the arms, expected "that those nations which have proved their ability in the past as leaders of science and mechanical engineering will in the future be those which will produce the most efficient armies" (1920: 310). Fuller was confident, but struggling to secure the tank arm. A total of 34 tank battalions (and one armoured car battalion) had been authorized for an offensive in June 1919, of which 26 were raised by the armistice, including 18 deployed (Fuller 1920: 65-66). All were deleted or reduced to cadres, until four were reinstated from 1922 to 1923 (plus a nominal unit serving as Depot; later, Tank Corps Centre). In October 1923, the arm was made permament (as the Royal Tank Corps).

Structural renewal belied regression in the equipment. In 1923, the only tanks in service were Heavy Mark Vs and Medium Cs. Production of Medium Ds ended in 1921, after ten vehicles, of four series. None was armed with more than machine-guns, as the design authority prioritized mobility and resisted user requirements for Male versions (see Table 5). This design authority was known, from April 1919, as the Tank Design & Experimental Department, Ministry of Munitions. Materially, this was a remnant, much reduced and consolidated, of the wartime Tank Corps' experimental workshops, under Colonel Philip Johnson. He always specialized in running gear, and proved to be the wrong person to lead the design of whole tanks.

A Medium D Modified, delivered in 1921.

The Vickers Independent in 1926.

He pursued ever faster, lighter vehicles, which he hoped to spin off as civilian tractors and carriers in private ventures. In 1921, the Ministry was abolished, and TD&E was given to the MGO. Johnson finally got around to designing a turreted Medium Male, as required, but not with enough conviction to prevent the MGO cancelling all Medium Ds in July 1922. A few months later, the MGO abolished TD&E, effective at the end of March 1923 (end of the fiscal year). Experimentation with legacy mediums was terminated on 10th August 1924. All 126 tanks from Medium B to Medium D Modified were scrapped, except two of each type reposed at Bovington (although these were scrapped in the 1930s) (War Office, GS(W)1(c), "The Medium D Tank," 3rd May 1946, RACTM E2011.530).

All the private suppliers dropped out after completing reduced contracts in 1919. The world's largest armaments firm (Vickers) had not designed or assembled tanks in wartime, but wanted to hedge against any decline in other business. Its automotive subsidiaries got involved in assembling some of the Medium Ds, while Vickers hired government technicians. By 1921, it started to offer light tanks. Its third type was delivered for trials in October 1923, and accepted into service as the Light Tank Mark I in 1924. With the cancellation of Mediums A to D, the Vickers Light was reclassified as Medium. Finally, the Army had a tank with a revolving turret, and a Medium with armament heavier than machine-guns, but the Vickers tank was the thinnest-armored and tallest tank in British service to date.

As far as the users knew, the Light/Medium was a stop-gap. The War Office's Superintendent of Design at Woolwich Arsenal (focused on firearms and carriages) developed light and medium tracked tractors (Dragons) and a tank based on the Medium Dragon (Project A3, piloted in 1926 as a "machine-gun carrier"), followed by larger, better-armed mediums (A7 series, piloted from 1929).

Meanwhile, Vickers was cooperating with this department on a heavy tank, which was piloted in 1926 as A1E1, "Independent." Compared to prior heavies, it was better armed and armored, faster, and almost as good at crossing obstacles. Its innovations included laryngophones and mechanical target indicators from the commander's station to all five turrets. It was rejected, nominally on cost, which was driven partly by Vickers' monopolization. Vickers was engaged at the same time on a new light tank (1929) and a series of "sixteen-tonners" (A6E1 and A6E2 in 1927; A6E3 and Medium Mark IIIE1 and E2 in 1929; Medium Mark IIIE3 in 1931).

A Vickers Medium Mark Ia, delivered in 1925.

The Superintendent of Design's A3E1, as piloted in 1926.

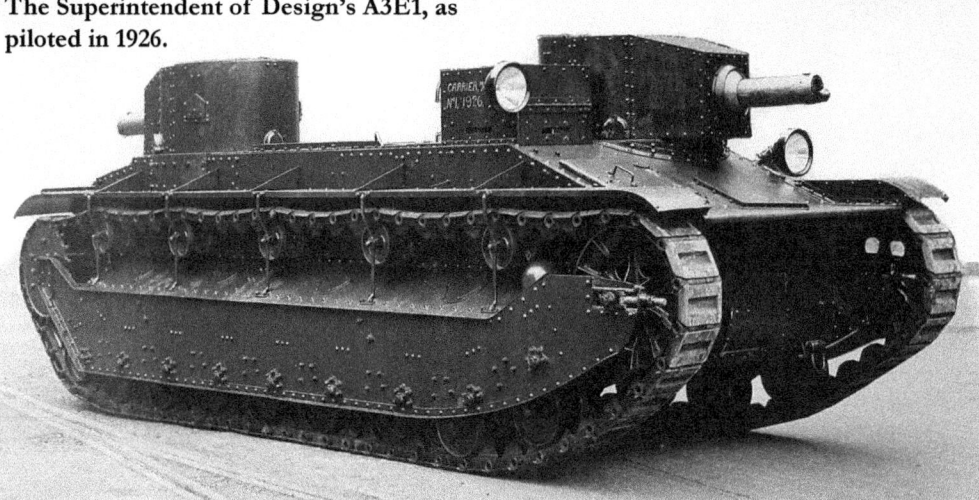

The Superintendent of Design's A7E1 in 1929.

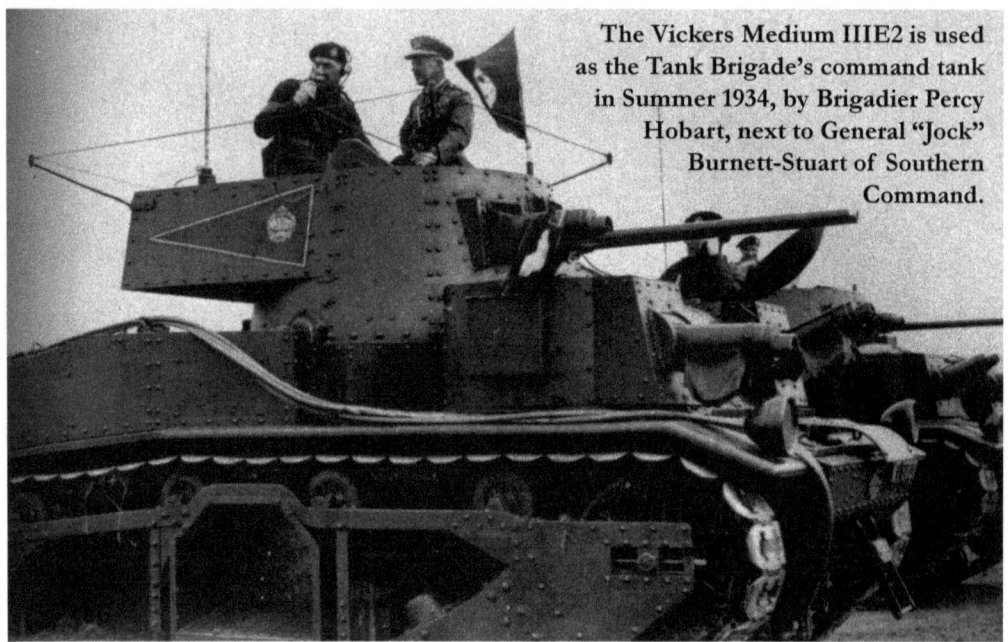

The Vickers Medium IIIE2 is used as the Tank Brigade's command tank in Summer 1934, by Brigadier Percy Hobart, next to General "Jock" Burnett-Stuart of Southern Command.

In May 1927, the commander of the Tank Corps Centre (Colonel-Commandant T.C. Mudie) lectured to the Staff College with optimism:

> I would like to remind you that when estimating the rate of advance likely to be achieved, it is as well to remember that, although in tank gunnery we are dependent for development on our own and Naval thought, as regards the development of the amount of protection given by a certain weight of steel, and of speed and power produced by the I.C. [internal combustion] engine, we have behind us the brains and experiences of two of the greatest industries of the country working at these problems for their own ends, and we may therefore expect developments in these matters to be rapid and continuous even in peace, when little money is available from Army funds to stimulate research. (Mudie 1927: 141)

In February 1929, the Secretary of State for War (Sir Laming Worthington-Evans) justified the annual "Army Estimates" (budget request) to Parliament with the claim that "We have carried out experiments and research on a large scale, and with such success that we can confidently claim to lead the world not only in our equipment of tanks but also in our ideas as to their use in war."

Fall

However, although the Army and War Office were producing the best doctrines and requirements, the government was not buying the tanks to meet them. The four units required 196 tanks in peacetime: only 160 Vickers Light/Medium tanks were delivered by 1928. The rest of the Army remained largely pedestrian and equestrian. In November 1927, Fuller complained that "we still have an infantry army…For just on 11 years I have written and lectured on this subject, not that it has been a profitable task…The other arms have been so reduced in strength since 1918 as to be incapable of independent action" (1928: viii, 30). His former wartime colleague (Giffard le Quesne Martel) had just commanded a unit of engineers in the first Experimental Mechanized Force, from which he emerged more optimistic:

> Just as we were the first to develop and use tanks in the Great War, so we have been the first to take the next step and develop a mechanized force, and with our present start we should be able to maintain our lead ahead of other nations. ("The present position as regards Mechanisation," enclosed to George Lindsay, 9th February 1928, RACTM E2004.3465)

In May 1929, George Lindsay, outgoing Inspector of the Royal Tank Corps (IRTC), wrote to DSD: "We have not got one single tank of any description that is fit for war...Therefore the first thing we must do is to rearm the Royal Tank Corps throughout, otherwise we may be caught a few years hence with our present tanks, and the whole tank idea wrecked through the complete failure of our equipment."

F. Elliot Hotblack, formerly the intelligence officer in the wartime Tank Corps, was one of Lindsay's staff officers: "the difficulties in training an armored brigade are, in some measure, an advantage since we are well ahead of other nations in this respect, and we can feel confident that no one else can produce a well-trained armored brigade 'out of a hat' at short notice." However, Hotblack warned that Britain would be overtaken unless it restored its capacity of the early 1920s ("Notes on medium armored brigade exercise 4 September 1930," RACTM Lindsay RTC).

Later, Martel would recall 1929 as the high point:

> After the war they had to struggle for seven years against retrograde views, but from 1926 to 1929 their views were accepted and we led the world in the development of modern mobile warfare. After that the financial depression occurred and stopped all progress, and we watched Germany copying all our methods and gaining ground, whereas we could easily have remained a long way ahead. (to The Times, 11th August 1950)

Martel was a hypocrite. He had championed tanks as large as warships, others with capacity for just one man and a machine-gun. He demonstrated his own one-man "tank" in August 1925 (right), but the army classified the type as "tankette." The term "tank" was applied to turreted, tracked AFVs, upon acquisition of the Vickers Light/Medium in 1924. Tankettes are the worthy subject of a different book. For this book's purposes, note that Martel and Basil Liddell Hart, then military correspondent at *The Daily Telegraph*, advocated tankettes as most cost-effective, for all arms. They claimed that tankettes could go where the current arms could not (in fact, they could not cross the same obstacles) and could swarm but not be targeted (in fact, they were half as quick as cavalry, less lethal than artillery, and less survivable than tanks). In December 1927, the first Director of Mechanization (Capel Peck) abolished the term "tankette" and reclassified its requirements as carriers and tractors (Peck 1929).

Nevertheless, as the suppliers exported more tankettes, home requirements also tended smaller and lighter. Vickers became monopolistic after acquiring Carden-Loyd (the most successful of the tankette suppliers), but less innovative. Ground vehicles remained a minor concern; exports became more important than home orders; and procurers became less ambitious. In 1929, Vickers delivered the first in a long evolutionary series of light tanks. This scores well in effectiveness for

This Matilda I is still in trials in July 1939.

the 1920s, given high speed and small size (see Graph 3). However, it was really a two-man scout tank, armed with one machine-gun. It was procured initially for the cavalry, but would be pressed on the RTC in lieue of other tanks. This helps to explain why the series spawned three-man versions in the 1930s, but only with machine-guns. War proved it useful for only scouting and supporting infantry.

In 1930, Vickers delivered the last 20 of its 200 Lights/Mediums (IIa). The last upgrade (II**) was not complete until 1935. None improved lethality, survivability, or reliability. The only other mediums in service were the six 16-tonners, of which Mark IIIE1 broke its steering in June 1934 and burnt out in 1935. Steering was one objection to further acquisition. The Vickers Lights/Mediums remained the only "mediums" in British service until import of US M3 Mediums in 1941.

In 1931, the Superintendent of Design was authorized to form a section for tracked and fighting vehicles (DDM), initially to research and design parts. Soon, DDM was developing whole tanks, including a superior light tank (L4E1, piloted 1937) and a medium tank (A7E3, piloted 1934), although neither was issued.

One reason was confused requirements. The infantry acquired tankettes as machine-gun carriers, and required tanks to be optimized to support pedestrian assaults. The RTC agreed to support other arms, but preferred independent strike operations. It was using machine-gun carriers and light tanks in lieu of medium tanks, in all roles. The Cavalry used light tanks for scouting and pursuit. The Army procured more lights and carriers than any other class in every year of the 1930s.

Martel, almost as soon he took over as Assistant Director of Mechanization in 1936, split the unfulfilled medium requirement into two new classes: infantry tanks (to support the infantry in the assault) and cruiser tanks (to exploit the breach). The requirements had been aired before, and were common abroad. The problem was that Martel initially specified only machine-guns for infantry tanks. Thus, the first infantry tank (Matilda I) was a thickly armored two-man tank. The IRTC (Percy Hobart) wanted multi-turreted mediums, but Martel wanted them fast. Sticking to the interwar convention that engines should be commercially available, both types

Two Cruiser IIs lead a Valentine I and two Matilda IIs at a RAOC Depot in August 1940.

ended up under-powered, so he could not specify as much armor or armament as the RTC wanted. Then he split the cruisers into two sub-classes: light cruisers, with 15 mm of armor, at best; and heavy cruisers, with up to 30 mm, to give closer support to the infantry. Further, each was required with a Close Support version, armed with a small howitzer to fire smoke and (to a lesser extent) high explosive.

In November 1936 the British imported a M1930 chassis from Walter Christie of New Jersey (designated A13E1 in Britain). Morris Motors was contracted to deliver a derivative (A13E2), without arrangements for track-less running and steering, with a turret by DDM. After trials (October 1937), a new derivative (A13E3) was ordered with improved tracks and drive. Given trials (from February 1938), minor development was specified before mass production (as the A13 Mark I Cruiser, or Cruiser Mark III). Deliveries started in March 1939, in the same month as Vickers got its Cruiser I (A9) into mass production, before its Cruiser II (A10) (December).

Meanwhile, DDM and Vulcan Foundry derived from the A7E3 an infantry tank, piloted in 1938, the same year as Vickers piloted the Matilda I. The superior tank (with a 40-mm gun and three men in the turet) was piloted as A12E1, and later standardized as Matilda II. However, poor resourcing curbed mass production before the Second World War. Thus, Vickers earned orders for an inferior infantry tank as stop gap (Valentine: a slightly better protected Cruiser II). More perversely, the Valentine would be developed in wartime with larger guns and thicker armor, but not the Matilda II. The Valentine became the most produced platform in both Britain and Canada during the war, which is perhaps the best single indicator of how poorly the interwar period ended for the British (Newsome 2016).

Realization

Basil Liddell Hart, as military correspondent for *The Daily Telegraph* and (from 1935) *The Times* (the two newspapers closest to government), was best placed to raise alarm about the British Army's relative decline. For instance, he wrote in 1931:

The British Army, after beginning its post-war career with a cry of "Back

(From top) The Christie M1930/A13E1, Morris-DDM A13E2, and Morris-DDM A13E3 were first tried in November 1936, October 1937, and February 1938 respectively.

to 1914," has actually advanced some way along the road signposted in 1918. It was the first to be equipped with high-speed tanks, the first to use tanks independently of infantry, the first to adopt six-wheeled cross-country transport; it formed the first completely mechanized force, and issued the first official manual of mechanized warfare. Even so, its practice has not kept pace with its theory. Its mechanized units, if modern in idea, are undeveloped in figure, and it has done nothing yet to rid itself of its adipose tissue of infantry. Its leaders put off the fateful decision by continuing experiments which have already yielded all the proof that is possible...The popular idea of "Britain's Mechanized Army" is a delusion. There has been much activity of thought and experiment, but little has yet been done to apply it by re-equipping the Army as a whole. (Liddell Hart 1932: 126, 169)

Liddell Hart became more vociferous in 1932:

There is scarcely a thoughtful soldier today, certainly among those who had front-line experience in the last war, who does not privily confess that our five existing divisions are hardly better than "suicide clubs." How can it be otherwise when the scale of infantry stopping power – of machine-guns and light automatics – has increased everywhere, while the scale of infantry supporting power – of guns and tanks – has greatly decreased since 1918? (Liddell Hart 1933: 109)

However, Liddell Hart was part of the problem. While he fairly advocated for mechanization, he prioritized tankettes (interchangeably with "light tanks"), light artillery, machine-guns, bombers, and (most of all) fortifications (1935: 245).

The editors of rival newspapers properly focused on tanks:

Since the war the British have hitherto kept their lead in tank design. We have the fastest and most efficient tanks in the world. But the British Army has only a few. For several years past the British industry has kept itself alive by selling tanks to other countries. ("Blunder that added two years to the War," The Daily Express, 17th September 1933)

Fuller noted that Britain had started with the most capacity for mechanization, but been overtaken. He dated the nadir to 1933, before the Tank Brigade was made permanent in 1934. He wanted more tank brigades (1935: 188-189), but the second would not be established until 1939. In April 1935, General John Burnett-Stuart, whose Southern Command administered the Tank Brigade, wrote to the CIGS with concerns about the Army's "compete unfitness" for war. On 31st October, he added proof from mobilization against Italian threats in Africa, and annual maneuvers at home, that the "army in any case is out of date, not only in equipment and material, but in organization and in the conception of its tasks." ("Postscript," LHCMA)

In July 1936, the Chief Instructor RTC Schools (Justice Tilly) complained:

The Great British Public don't yet know how disarmed we are, or what a vacillating policy of re-armament there is. If ever they do, there will be no ordinary volcano. One bright spot is the Air Force; I believe they know what they want, have got the money for it, and are getting it. The tragedy is, there is plenty of money for the Army, but no-one knows what to spend it on. (Tilly to Lindsay, 12th July 1936, in RACTM Lindsay)

Light Mark VI and Medium Mark II tanks on Salisbury Plain in August 1938.

In September 1936, Hobart reflected on the three annual training seasons through which the Tank Brigade had passed since permanent establishment:

> Some years ago it was generally acknowledged that the Royal Tank Corps led the world's tank forces in the same way as the Royal Navy did the sea forces. It is admitted by the most modern tank forces on the continent that they built themselves up on the model of the Royal Tank Corps. The Royal Tank Corps has now completely lost the lead in the matter of numbers, up-to-date equipment – and now retains superiority, if at all, only in maintenance, organization and tactical methods, and personnel. As to numbers: during these last three years our potential enemies have increased enormously their tank corps. In the Royal Tank Corps no increase has taken place. ("Tank Brigade Report, 1936," LHCMA Hobart)

Hobart blamed "ancient equipment" and "shortage of personnel."

> It may not be possible to regain our lost supremacy in tank design. But the equipment of the British Army with machines at least as efficient as continental ones is desirable...It is possible that as regards tactical methods and control we may still be somewhat in advance of continental nations, but we shall not be able to maintain the lead unless assistance is given. The inadequate peace establishments of Royal Tank Corps units make it impossible to man tanks with complete crews. This has very deleterious effects on training for war. The most modern Tank Corps on the continent have been given the pick of the officers and personnel of their armies. Prospects of promotion are good. Service in tank formations is a recommendation for higher appointments. Tanks are regarded as corps d'elite and everything is done to emphasize the fact.

The few advocates for rearmament in Parliament were most concerned with bombers. For instance, on 12th November 1936, Winston Churchill spoke from the back benches, over-estimating the German air force at more than 1,500 aircraft (the number that the British government aimed to acquire by March 1937). He wanted even more aircraft and anti-aircraft guns (which were manned by the army). His speech contained one complaint about tanks, for which he blamed the War Office:

> Look at the Tank Corps. The tank was a British invention. This idea, which has revolutionised the conditions of modern war, was a British idea

forced on the War Office by outsiders. Let me say they would have just as hard work today to force a new idea on it. I speak from what I know. During the War we had almost a monopoly, let alone the leadership, in tank warfare, and for several years afterwards we held the foremost place. To England all eyes were turned. All that has gone now. Nothing has been done in "the years that the locust hath eaten" to equip the Tank Corps with new machines. The medium tank which they possess, which in its day was the best in the world, is now looking obsolete. Not only in numbers – for there we have never tried to compete with other countries – but in quality these British weapons are now surpassed by those of Germany, Russia, Italy and the United States.

Fuller's complaints were more technically informed:

[In the Great War] we built up the most powerful tank force possessed by any belligerent, and it proved itself to be the master land arm. In spite of this, for 18 years now we have done next to nothing to develop this arm. We have been waiting for mechanical perfection (so the excuse has been) before going into production, and what is our position today? The USSR has the finest tank force in the world. There are machines in that country [BT7 tanks] which are capable of a road speed of 70 miles an hour, whilst most of our medium tanks are 14 years old. Every great power and also a number of secondary powers are ahead of us in this arm (1937: 212).

In November 1937, Burnett-Stuart submitted his final report, taking advantage of freedom from consequences, given retirement in 1938:

I have no wish to harp on the unpreparedness of the Regular Army for war. But I have once again, and for the last time, to report that there is no major unit and no formation in my command which is fit to take the field against the troops of a first-class military power...[The Tank Brigade] had not one medium tank fit for war; all the available medium tanks have long passed their official span of life. ("Annual Report on Training of the Regular Army, 1936/1937," November 1937, LHCMA Burnett-Stuart)

In the same month, Hotblack returned from serving as military attaché in Berlin, to take over the General Staff's department for armored fighting vehicles:

It is worth considering again the factors which are enabling the German Army not only to expand very rapidly but to produce a series of new and improved equipments and organizations. Germany has already made good the lean years in which she was held (more or less) under the limitations of the Treaty of Versailles, and there is every indication that this progress will continue, and it is an accepted standard in the German Army that no vehicle should remain in the service more than five years. (Many vehicles appear to be discarded or passed to reserve within an even shorter space of time.) ("New German Mechanized Formation," LHCMA Lindsay)

At the end of 1937, the WO's Mechanization Board noted Britain's relegation.

During the past year most nations have been giving a great deal more attention to the design and construction of armored fighting vehicles. In many cases the development that has taken place has been the outcome of several years' work on trial and research. The result is that whereas we were considered the leading nation in this work four or five years ago, other nations have spent so much money on research and production that they have now reached much the same position as ourselves in many respects and have reduced our lead very considerably. ("Fourth Report of the Mechanization Board Covering the Period 1st January 1937 to 31st December 1937": 3, RACTM MH4 E2010.1054)

Frederick Pile (Assistant Director of Mechanization from 1928-1932) realized "a tragic thought that whereas in 1930 we led the world in tank design, equipment, and development, by 1937 we were just an 'also ran'." (to Liddell Hart, 26th August 1948, LHCMA) Lieutenant-Colonel Douglas Portway, a Royal Engineer, lectured in 1940 that "nothing was done till about 1936, by which time our former lead in tank design had been completely lost." (Portway 1940: 23, 37) Another Royal Engineer added: "Although the first tanks were designed and made in England, although Great Britain for some time led the world in their conception and construction, the post-war years saw that lead lost and – worse still – lightly and carelessly forgone." (Gorman 1941: 22) A third engineer agreed: "The tank was invented and developed in Britain," but the Germans followed "our example," while "we stripped ourselves of armaments," apart from "paper" designs (Low 1941: 7). Cyril Falls, one of CID's historians during the 1930s, recalled that by 1936 "we had lost our lead in tank design and possessed very little equipment of any value in this arm." ("Tanks in Theory and Practice," The Times, 23rd September 1940: 5)

In 1938, Major E.W. Sheppard of the Royal Tank Corps wrote that "'the years that the locusts have eaten' have for the British RTC been longer and more barren than they need have been, or should have been allowed to be...In tank construction we have lost our first wartime supremacy" (Sheppard, 1938: 81, 125). At the same time, Major G.C. Shaw of the RAOC, which sustained fighting vehicles, warned Westerners against complacencies born of the Great War:

> During those years the Allies had it all their own way, so far as the tank went; they had little to fear that the enemy might suddenly produce in the field a tank more powerful and faster than their own. In a future conflict between nations, equally matched in their industrial resources, there will undoubtedly be keen competition in design, to gain superiority in battle. Here for the supply officer will be yet further difficulties; for time and space calculations, instead of being based on the standard performance of man and beast, which within small limits has not changed, will depend on the skill of the engineer and the output of the factory. (Shaw 1938: 165)

Lieutenant-General Philip Neame became deputy chief of staff to the new BEF in September 1939, almost 20 years since he was appointed to one of the first BEF's new Tank Groups (each with 12 tank units and 720 tanks).

> By 1918 we had invented the tank as a new weapon of war, and delivered vast attacks with great armored forces, the equivalent of two or three of the modern armored divisions, on one battle-front. All this knowledge and organization were lost and forgotten...Our armored force in 1919 would have been the equivalent of seven armored divisions of 1939-1945...
> But after the war the German Army absorbed the lesson, and from 1935

A Cruiser IV of 10th Hussars, 1AD, knocked out near Huppy, France, on 25th May 1940.

onward built up a great armored army, which, however, by 1939 had no more tanks than our 1919 army would have had. Our reactionary military thought, led by some of our Generals and encouraged by our political leaders, who formulated wishful policy of peace based on a false idea of the power of the League of Nations, dropped the armored idea almost entirely. (Neame 1947: 251, 79)

General Henry "Jumbo" Wilson, who was commanding British Troops in Egypt at the start of war, pondered "the necessity to think big when considering future developments; we did not do so in the pre-war years, yet we were the pioneers of armored fighting vehicles in the First World War." (Wilson 1950: 258)

Colonel Gordon MacLeod Ross, DDM's leading designer, wrote "that failure did not occur on the afternoon of 10th May 1940, when German tanks penetrated the Netherlands and Belgium, but over the twenty-two years since 1918" (Ross, 1976: 84). Winston Churchill became Prime Minister on 10th May, when, as he later put it, "Britain, the birthplace of the tank, had only just completed the formation and training of her first armored division (328 tanks), which was still in England." (Churchill 1949: 31) On 20th May 1940, as Western Allied forces retreated, Liddell Hart wrote for the *Evening Standard* newspaper about German import of Britain's "conception of qualitative warfare" of the 1920s.

> Yet their conception is not such a novelty as it may appear to most of our statemen and public. It is merely an advance to the stage which was reached by our more advanced military thinkers soon after the last war. What the German command has done is to put into practice ideas from which it was not too proud to learn, whereas our own authorities, distrusting them as untried "theories," considered it safer to keep in the familiar rut. There is nothing so unsafe, for a nation, as military conservatism. (Liddell Hart 1941: 322)

On 2nd June, writing for the same newspaper, he credited Fuller and Hobart:

> Once the German armored forces were through the crust of the French defences, their rapid and confusion-spreading advance fulfilled the predictions that Colonel Fuller and other British pioneers of mechanized warfare had made years ago. As for their technique, it seems to have followed the lines worked out in 1934 by our first modern tank brigade under Brigadier Hobart. It has been left to the Germans, unfortunately, to prove how practical they were. (Liddell Hart 1941: 338).

In a different newspaper, he started the myth that he had urged heavier tanks:

> The Germans...made haste to apply the new ideas which had been evolved in this country....It is a grim reflection that until some 10 years ago we led the world in tank design and in the conception of mechanized warfare – thanks to certain of the younger minds in the British Army ("Captain Hart Answers Lincolnshire General," Lincolnshire Echo, 3rd June 1940: 3).

On 14th June 1940, Lieutenant-General James Marshall-Cornwall's II Corps came under the command of French 10th Army, with responsibility for the nascent 1st Armored Division, which was then undertaking its final retreat. He spontaneously wrote some lessons learned for the Chief of the Imperial General Staff:

> Since the last war the British Army has never developed and insisted on an attack doctrine. British officers did not really believe that attacking infantry could successfully assault an organized position defended with automatic weapons. At the same time we paid so little attention to the requirements of continental warfare that even six months after the outbreak of war we had not one armored division ready for action. (Marshall-Cornwall 1984: 155-156)

In June 1941, Hobart (now commander of the nascent 11th Armoured Division) told his officers that "Germans seldom invented anything. They are adept at taking other people's ideas and developing them logically and thoroughly to their opponent's utmost confusion. The tank was a British invention. The modern method of using tanks...was copied and developed by the Germans." (RACTM E1968.30.5)

Writers of a new textbook on the Army noted that "the reapers [of British tank developments] were to be the Germans and not the Allies. France and Britain, who in 1919 had the largest air force and tank fleet in the world, in the next two decades allowed them to decay amid dreams of world peace." (Anonymous 1942: 84)

A newspaper editor later complained that "in the 20 years that followed [the Great War] we let the fruits of our experience go to rot." (Simon Harcourt-Smith, "The Great Tank Mystery," Daily Mail, 24th March 1944: 2) A war correspondent added that "we forgot and abandoned our original invention, and let the enemy – the same enemy – get away with it, and smash through Europe and North Africa before we put it into mass production." (Gibbs 1946: 192-193) Martel had "no doubt that our country initiated these thoughts [on armored warfare] and led the world in progress on these lines for many years." (1945: 17) A wartime tank commander wondered why "tactically and quantitatively the British Army's tank forces in 1939 compared unfavorably with those of Germany even though the equipping of the Wehrmacht had started almost from scratch in 1933." (Beale 1998: 38)

David Fletcher (1991: viii), Historian at the Tank Museum, wrote that "the years between the wars were the truly formative years. With very little past experience to guide them but massive technological strides to carry them on their way, the designers had free rein. Nearly every idea, no matter how bizarre, was developed at least to prototype state and evaluated, and more often than not found wanting, but it resulted in the appearance of some amazing armored vehicles that deserve to be recorded for their own sake."

J.P. Harris, another British historian, noted that "until the early 1930s Great Britain was widely regarded as the world leader in mechanized warfare doctrine, in tank design[,] and in the training and tactical handling of mechanized formations" (1995: 202). Brian Bond dated the end of the British Army's leadership to the "early 1930s" (1980: 34). John Mearsheimer dated the end to "the late 1930s, and Britain would go into World War II largely unprepared to engage the Wehrmacht" (1988: 22). Bryan Perrett found that Britain was the "intellectual" leader of armored warfare in that period, but the "real beneficiary of these ideas was the German Army" (1995: 67). Colin Gray noted that in "the 1920s and into the early 1930s, Britain retained both a technical and a theoretical lead in the development of tanks" but "the British Army did not sustain its lead in the 1930s" (2012: 132).

Revisionism

The consensus was revised from the 1990s by new fields, "War Studies," "Peace Studies," "History of Science," and "Social History," which perversely claim to be "counter-revisionist" or "counter-orthodox." They claim to be specialized, but betray less rigor and more biases. A third perversity is that they claim to be outsiders, while dominating the military and defence academies since the mid-1990s. Tellingly, by then – as in the 1930s – the discourse was dominated by new threats, confused responses, contempt for the past, and revolutionary thinking. Self-interestedly, the new fields interpret Western policies of the 1930s as efficient and effective – for not rearming at the pace that supposedly bankrupted the West's enemies. Conservative governments of the time made the same claim, although the new fields posture as counter-Conservative.

For instance, Joseph Maiolo, Professor of War Studies at Kings College London, claimed to prove that the West won the arms race in the 1930s, but delivered a thick, chaotic book of anecdotes from the perspective of the national leaders of the time, without chronological or technical themes, without comparing acquisitions systems or armaments across nations. He marketed the anecdotes as "data," but his book contains no tables, graphs, figures, or appendices (Maiolo, 2010).

David Edgerton, writing while a historian of technology at Imperial College London, before moving to Kings College as a modern historian, also claimed to "revise" prior literature and to offer "new data," but delivered anecdotes. His most overarching claim was that Britain became a supremely productive and technologically superior "warfare state" once it adopted the centralized principles of the "welfare state" (2005). In fact, Britain did not declare a welfare state until after World War II. Focusing on that war, he claimed that Britain was actually ready in 1939. Ignoring the literature I have quoted above, he imagined a post-war "idea of a weak Britain which made a minor contribution to victory. The story became one of the defeat of a faltering power in 1940, which in one last heroic gesture bankrupted itself to save the world." (2011: 1) Fleetingly, he reveals his partisan bias when he imagines "declinist histories which indulged in inverted Whiggism, finding past failure to account for present decline," written by "British nationalists, militarists

A Bren Gun Carrier, as depicted in the War Office's "Photographs of Modern Equipments," officially issued on 8th November 1939.

and technocrats [who] imagined Germany as the template on which Britain should have built itself" (6-8). Hypocritically, he went on to criticize other interpretations as "parochial" and "ideological" (9). "In this book I deploy a new approach I have developed for the study of the material which considers all the machines and structures, whether old or new, celebrated or ignored, whether they figure in theories of modernity or not." (5-6) In fact, his book focuses on personalities. The "machines" are few and far between, selective, and misinterpreted. For instance, his claim that Britain had the best tanks in 1939 relies on re-categorizing its mediums as heavies, while re-categorizing German mediums as lights (63, 320).

James Holland, a broadcast historian, subsequently noted "a quiet revolution going on in academic circles," prompting him to reconsider the "general perception…that at the start of the war Nazi Germany had the best-trained army in the world with the best equipment and weapons." (2015: 2) However, he cited nobody. He declared that "the British Army was still the best equipped and most modern in the world." Yet his discussion of the British Army's equipment similarly cites no evidence, and covers less than 5 of the book's 700 pages. These 5 pages contain a litany of falsities: the British Expeditionary Force was "entirely mechanized"; its trucks were "rugged and robust" (in fact, they were unadapted commercial types); the arms used a "tracked troop carrier" (his mischaracterization of the Bren Gun Carrier); British soldiers received "the most modern and practical combat uniform adopted by any European power"; British infantry boasted more "firepower" and mobility than any foreign infantry; the cavalry was separate to "the newly formed Royal Armored Corps, which contained the new regiments of the Royal Tank Corps"; and "British tanks were, for the most part, on a par with, if not better than, German versions…[and] really not bad at all." (101-103) His chapter on the German Army went to only 8 pages, of which he spent 5 alleging that German Army clothing was costlier, more diverse, and less "modern" than British Army clothing (118-122). Tellingly, he offered no data on any of the German or Soviet tanks that cooperatively invaded Poland in September 1939.

The ridiculousness of revisionist claims will become clearer when we focus on German and Soviet developments, but in between we must consider what the other former Western Allies of the Great War developed before the Second World War.

CHAPTER 5

French proliferation, 1919-1939

French interwar tank development is somewhat contradictory. Legacy light (FT) and super-heavy platforms (Char 2c) continued to serve into the Second World War with little development. New light-medium (Char D) and heavy (Char B) series were developed, with advanced technologies (such as differential steering), but also regrettable choices (such as one-man turrets). Further, alot of redundant cavalry and infantry tanks were acquired in the 1930s.

Super-Heavy and Heavy tanks

FCM (*Forges et Chantiers de la Méditerranée*) ended the First World War with a heavy tank (*Char 2c*) in development, of which ten were completed from 1921 to 1923. Their armor (30-mm; 45-mm from 1931) and armament (75-mm gun and machine-gun in forward turret; machine-gun in rearward turret; a machine-gun in each side) were exceptional for their time. However, the platform was huge (for good trench-crossing), heavy (69 metric tons; 69 long; 76 short), slow (9 mph, even after upgrade to a 500 horsepower generator), and extravagant in crew (13 men).

In 1921, the French specified a new assault tank, this time to four commercial and publicly-owned bidders, but in a strange non-competitive accord (the Army would own all intellectual property). The pay-off would be to share production, but this hardly incentivized good design. The specifications did not help. Estienne was responsible for the requirement, specifications, and accord. He commanded the tank force until 1927, even though it had transferred from Artillery to Infantry in 1920. This transfer intensified the bias to infantry-support. Estienne's bias has been obscured by the term he used (*Char de Bataille*; "battle tank"), which has a different meaning today. Economizing was a factor, but is a factor in all peacetime projects.

One of five Char 2c tanks part-demolished on a blocked railway, on 15th June 1940.

A Char B1 leads a Bastille Day parade in Paris, 14th July 1937.

Weight was initially classified medium, although it would grow to heavy-medium, and eventually heavy. Most consequentially, the main armament was specified in the front of the hull, to save size and thence weight and cost. A machine-gun in a turret provided close defence. The occupant would need to command the tank too. To further save on size, the main armament was specified without traverse, which necessitated a fine steering system for aiming. This was the configuration that would curse French "heavy" tanks into World War II.

The preferred bid of 1924 was respecified and developed into three new pilots, now designated *Char B*. These were unhurriedly tested until the *Char B1* was specified in 1934, This had a 47-mm anti-tank gun in the turret, and a 75-mm howitzer in the front hull. (Each weapon had been mounted on respective pilots previously.) After delivery from December 1935, a development (*Char B1 bis*) was specified with 60-mm armor (instead of 40-mm), a higher-velocity 47-mm, and a more powerful engine. This was delivered in 1937, at the same time as the French specified a *Char B1 ter*, with 70-mm armor, a slightly more powerful engine, and slight traverse of the hull gun, so that the fine steering system could be dropped (on grounds of cost). The *Char B1 ter* was being piloted when the Germans defeated France in June 1940, at which point the French Army deployed 365 tanks in the *Char B* series (mostly *bis*). The platform offered better mobility on soft ground than other French tanks, due to wide tracks, many wheels, and tall running gear. However, it was slow, which exacerbated both the poor survivability of such a large vehicle and its poor command and gunnery arrangements (Tucker 2004: 58).

Light/Medium tanks

In the 1920s, the FT was developed in pursuit of more speed, although acquisitions were few. Kégresse fitted a reinforced rubber tracked running gear, while Renault tried different suspensions inspired by Kégresse's system (otherwise used on half-tracks). Renault's series of offerings (designated NC, for no reason) earned him an order in 1928 to develop something to fulfill a new *Char D* requirement. The excellence of the many French pilots of the 1920s can be appreciated in Graph 3.

The weight class was medium by British and US standards, although the French classified it as light. After some more pilots, and preseries production in 1930 (NC31), the definitive product (*Char D1*) was delivered from 1931 with a 47-mm instead of short 37-mm gun, and 40-mm instead of 30-mm armor. Compared to the Vickers Medium, the *Char D1* was much more survivable, just as lethal, more mobile across country, and almost as fast on road, for about the same weight and lower height. The *Char D2* (1936) gained an engine twice as powerful, more road wheels, and a more spacious turret (although the Char D turrets were little different to the Char B turrets). In 1938, a second series D2 was specified with a longer gun, although poor resourcing prevented fielding before early 1940.

Light tanks

One explanation for the poor resourcing of the Char D series is the procurement since 1930 of a plethora of light tanks for the cavalry, plus variants for the infantry. As in America, the infantry owned tanks, so the cavalry procured them as "combat cars" (*Automitrailleuse de Combat*; AMC) or "reconnaissance cars" (*Automitrailleuse de Reconnaissance*; AMR). The cavalry had previously used wheeled and half-tracked vehicles. Procurement was not competitive or swift: Renault developed the AMR33 in 1933 (from a Carden-Loyd carrier, with a turret for a single machine-gun), the AMC34 in 1935 (with a short 47-mm gun), the AMR35 in 1936 (like the AMR33, but with the engine moved to the rear, and improved suspension), a parallel AMR35 (with a 13.2-mm machine-gun), the AMC35 in 1938 (like AMC34, with slightly thicker armor, longer gun, and more power), and, at the cusp of 1939/1940, a new version of the AMR35 (with a 25-mm gun).

In their midst, Renault was ordered to deliver a "light tank" (*Char léger*) to support the infantry (R35). In the same year (1935), the Cavalry ordered from Hotchkiss a similar tank (H35), which the infantry had rejected. The infantry persisted with a bid from FCM, even though FCM delivered its first pilot late and short of

A Char D1, as delivered in 1936.

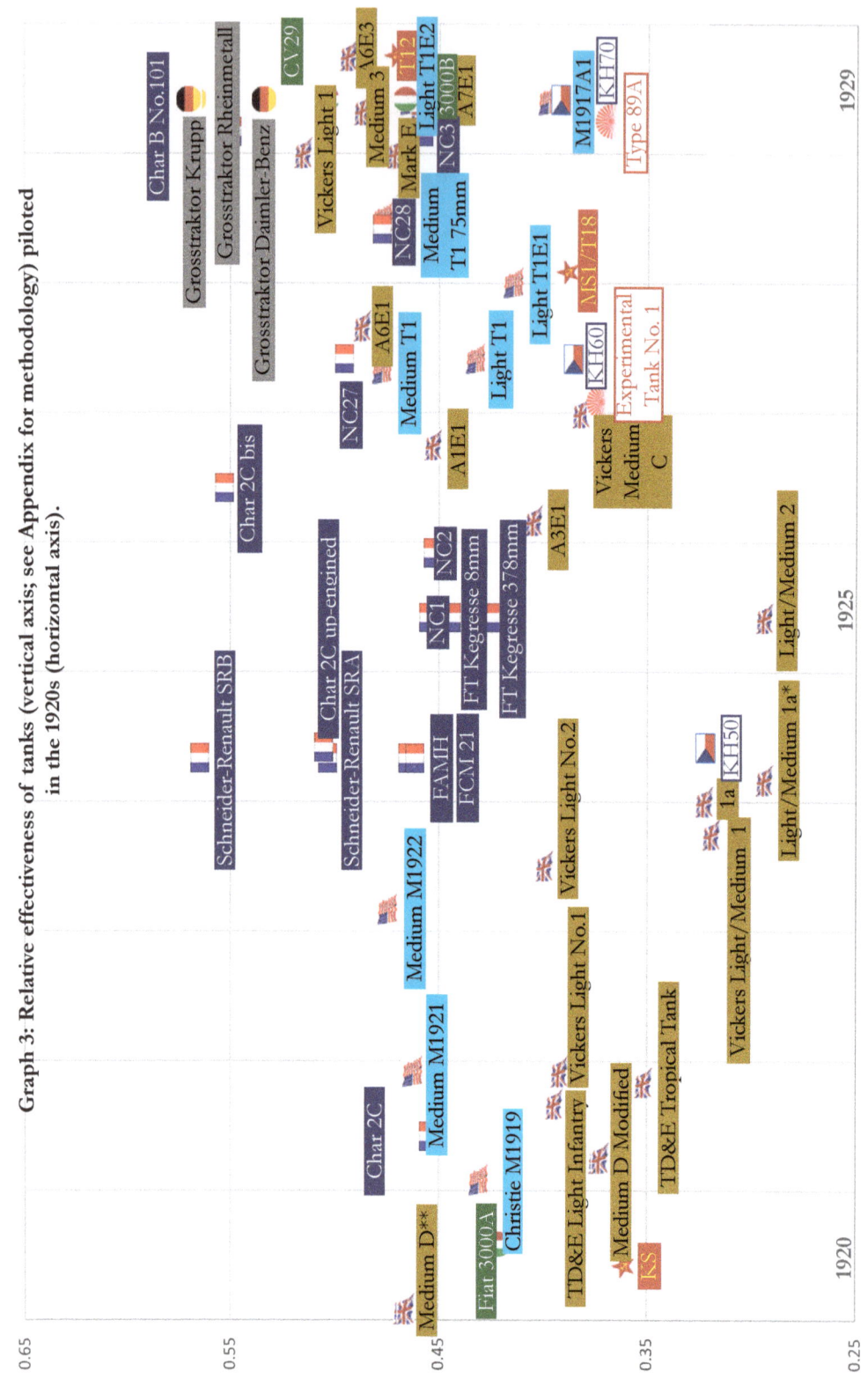

Graph 3: Relative effectiveness of tanks (vertical axis; see Appendix for methodology) piloted in the 1920s (horizontal axis).

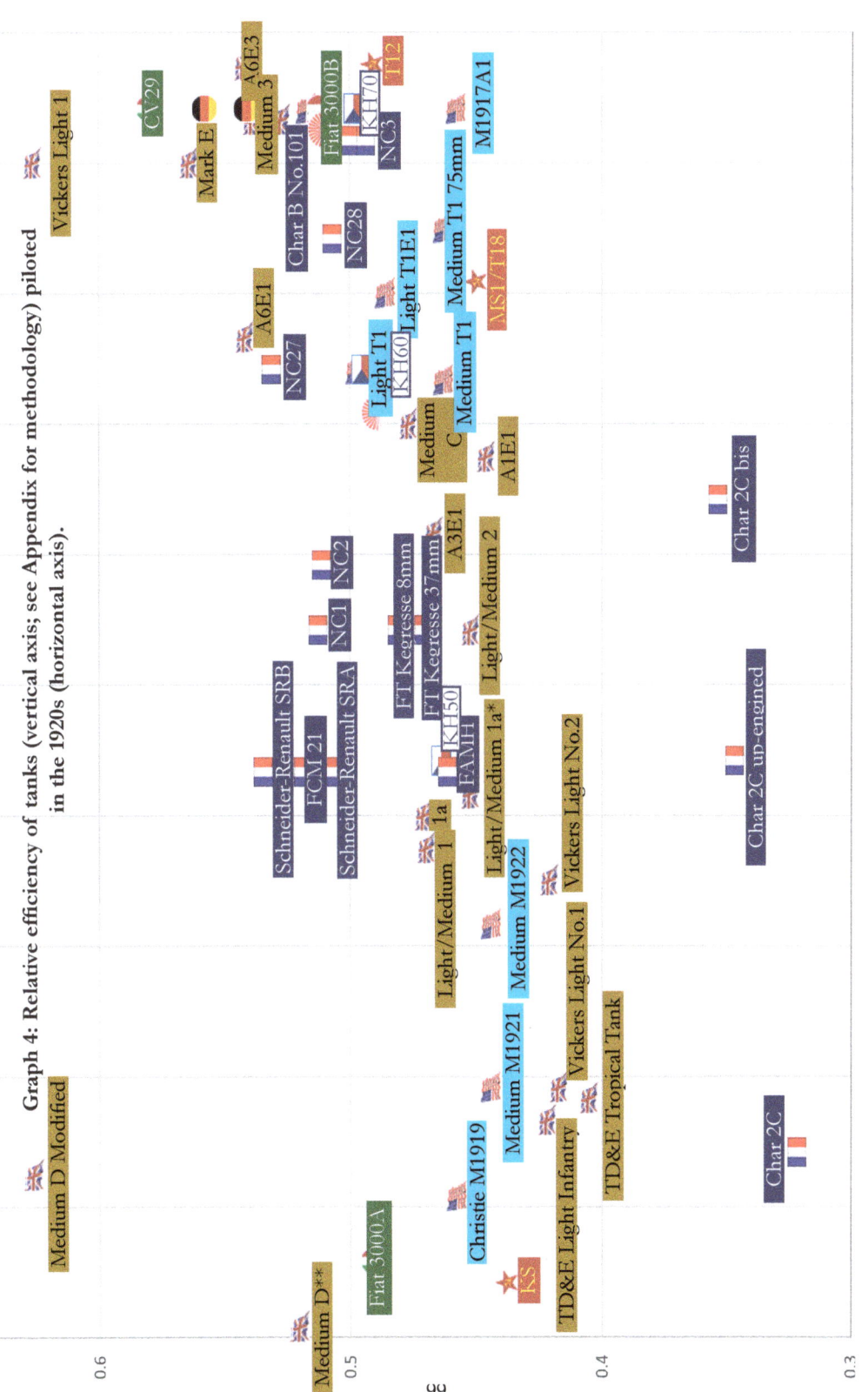

Graph 4: Relative efficiency of tanks (vertical axis; see Appendix for methodology) piloted in the 1920s (horizontal axis).

(Below) Renault's AMC35 of 1938.

(Right) Renault R35s in the Alps.

Hotchkiss H39s, in Spring 1940.

A Somua 35, as taken into service in early 1937.

specifications. This needed development into 1936 (FCM36), when it was declared the best, because of its sloped armor and diesel engine. Nevertheless, the other two went into production. All were well-armoured (40 mm) and -armed (37-mm gun) for their size and weight. However, size and weight were their only advantages over the Char Ds (which, let us not forget, were classified as lights). Each carried just two men (driver; commander/gunner/loader). None was faster than any of the Char Bs, until the H39 (effectively a H35 with a larger engine), at 22 mph (36.5 kmh).

Off-road performance remained poor, so in 1937 the infantry sponsored Renault to improve R35. More accurately, the infantry sponsored Renault's military subsidiary (*Atelier de Construction d'Issy-les-Moulineaux*; AMX), which had been nationalized (August 1936), along with spin-offs from Hotchkiss and Schneider. Nationalization enabled cross-fertilization across former competitors. The three arsenals (APX, ARE, ARL, named after respective locations: Puteaux, Roanne, Rueil) were given more tank business. ARL assembled the *Char B1 bis*, while APX designed the turrets (Ogorkiewicz 1970: 170; Chamberlain and Ellis 1972: 24-25; Ellis and Chamberlain 1975: 31). The R35 modification (1939) became a new version (R40) with a longer gun and a radio. Deliveries started in May 1940, in time to be issued to two units during invasion.

We have still not exhausted the French light tanks of the 1930s – twelve in this review. (For comparison: the British received six marks, and two lettered variants of the sixth, from 1929 to 1939.) The best (SOMUA S35) was developed mid-way through the decade, by an unrelated company, on a new platform, which adds to the mystery of why the others continued to be developed. The project dates from 1934, with specifications for a medium-weight AMC, issued to a subsidary of Schneider (*Société d'Outillage Mécanique et d'Usinage d'Artillerie*; SOMUA). The S35 was practically the same weight as the Char D2, carried the same turret, and matched it in armor and armament, but was faster (25 mph; 41 kmh), thanks to more power and superior running gear (helped by Skoda of Czechoslovakia, then developing the LT35). The commander could get help in operating the gun from the radio-operator, who was accomodated nearby, instead of next to the driver, as in the Char B and Char D series. Welding and sloped armor added to survivability. For some, it was "one of the finest armored fighting vehicles of its day" (Chamberlain and Ellis 1972: 39-40). Given mass production from January 1937, it could have become the main French type. However, less than 250 products were delivered by World War II. One excuse was expense, which sounded unpragmatic by wartime.

At root, France proliferated too many types, without fully abandoning the configuration choices made in the 1920s, such as the one-man turret. The relative decline of French tanks in the later 1930s can be appreciated in Graph 5.

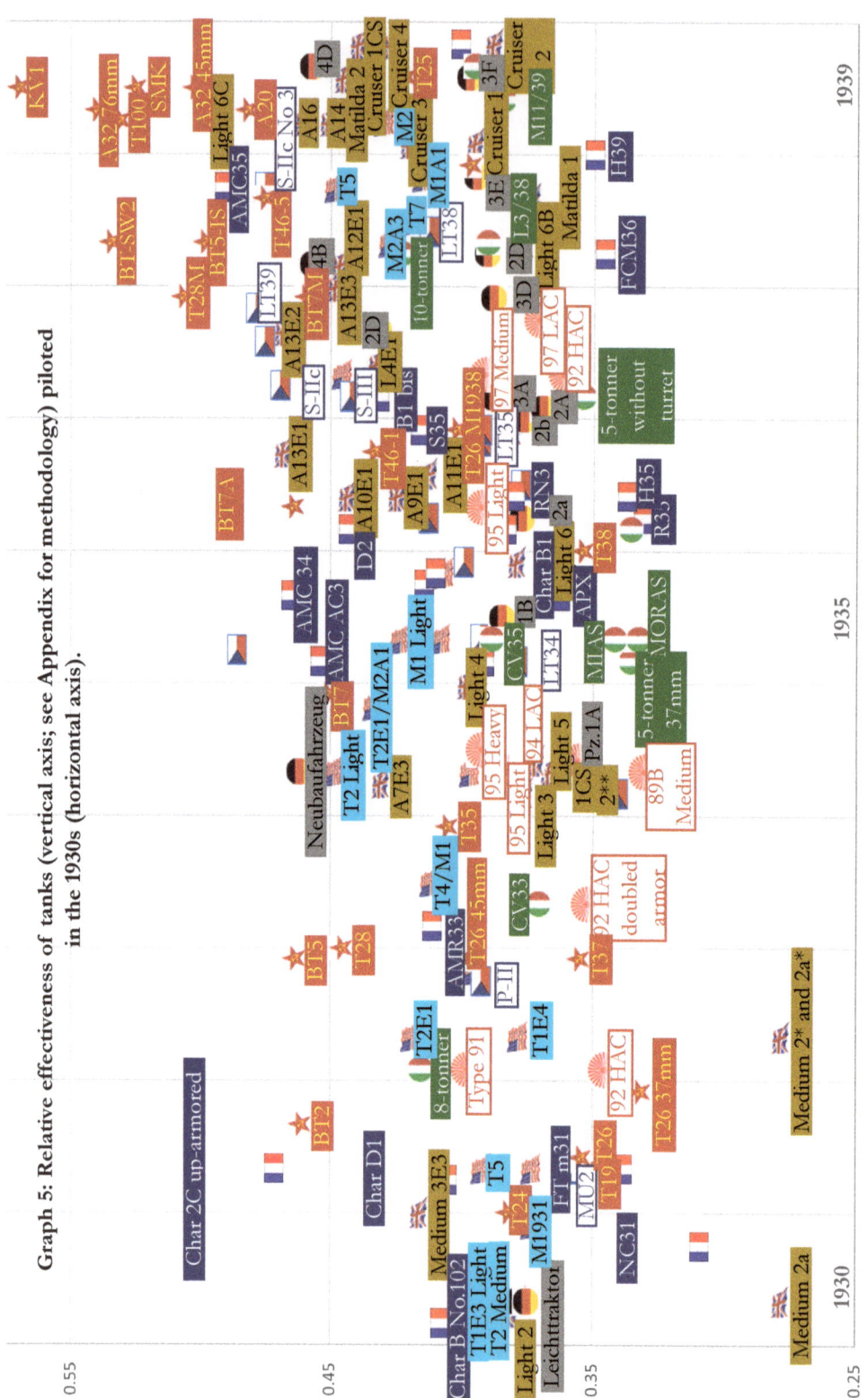

Graph 5: Relative effectiveness of tanks (vertical axis; see Appendix for methodology) piloted in the 1930s (horizontal axis).

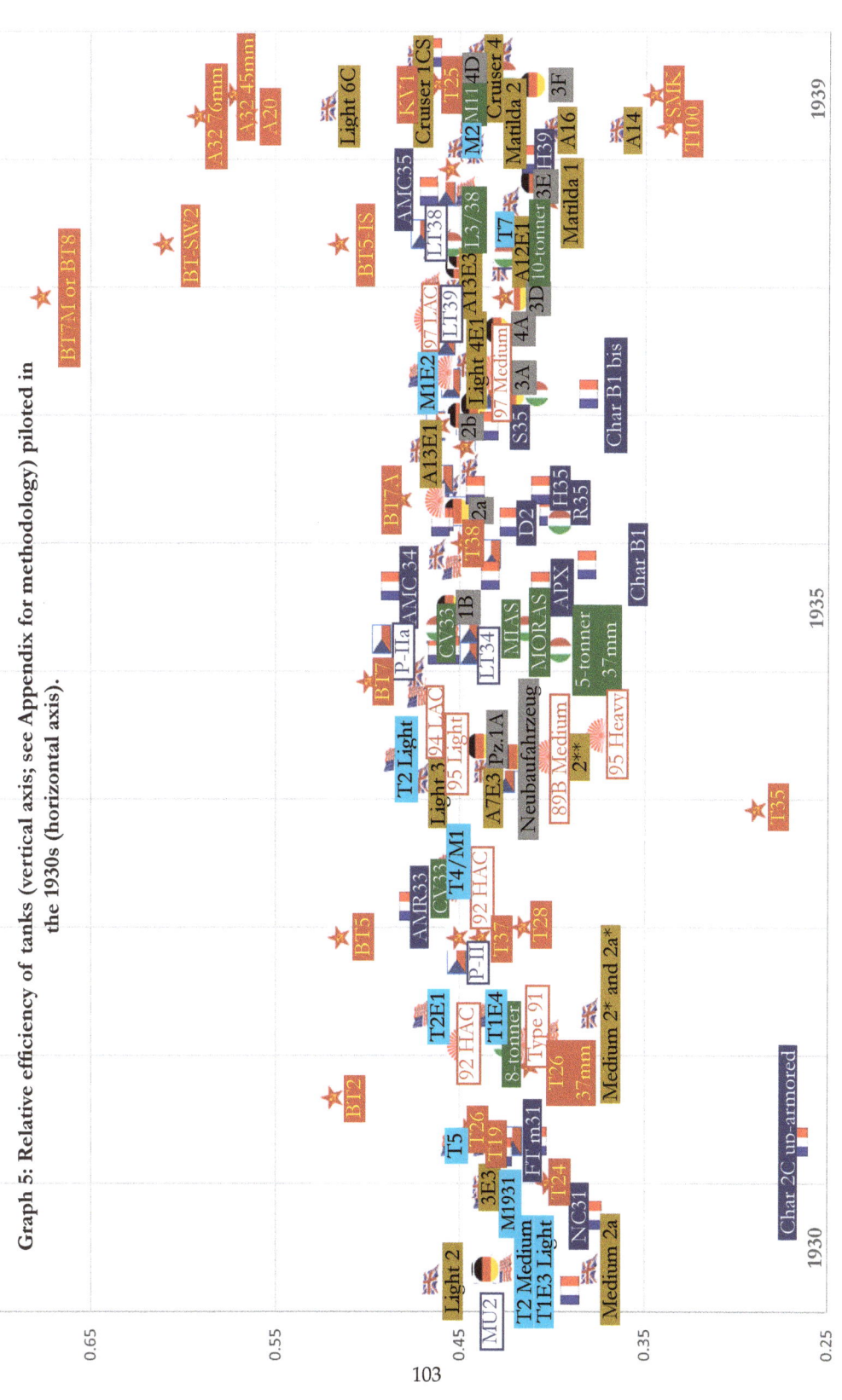

Graph 5: Relative efficiency of tanks (vertical axis; see Appendix for methodology) piloted in the 1930s (horizontal axis).

The T1 as delivered in 1927, with wooden mock-up turret and superstructure at the rear.

The T1E6, as delivered in 1932.

A M2A2 Light on maneuvers in Summer 1939.

CHAPTER 6

American under-ambition, 1919-1939

The US Army had left Europe with design authority over American versions of the best French light tank (FT) and British heavy tank (Mark VIII), and promises to try the latest British mediums. However, it wasted most of its efforts on light tanks.

Light tanks

In 1921, the Tank Corps was abolished and distributed to the infantry and cavalry, which tended to require ever lighter and faster tanks. Yet, even within the requirement for lighter and faster, the Americans neglected their own technologies.

Most notably, J. Walter Christie offered the fastest tanks in the world, with uniquely long suspension travel, large roadwheels, and convertibility from tracks to steerable and driven roadwheels. The Army tried all his tanks, from 1921 to 1938, and even developed its own with the same technology, but standardized tanks with inferior running gear. Certainly, the Ordnance Department was frustrated with Christie's unresponsiveness, particularly on turrets and armaments. Nevertheless, the Soviets, Poles, and British developed his platforms into tanks. Poorly compensated, he became increasingly eccentric, and died almost penniless in 1944.

The Ordnance Department's first peacetime light tank series was admirable, thanks to a public-private partnership between Rock Island Arsenal, Illinois, and James Cunningham, Son, & Co. of Rochester, New York. Ordnance's Proving Ground at Aberdeen, Maryland, was effectively involved in development. The T1 (piloted in 1927) looked like a lighter version of the Medium A. The T1E4 of 1932 looked like the Vickers six-tonner. For their size, the T1s were well armed (a 37-mm gun of different lengths), better armored than the Vickers lights and mediums (9.5 mm through T1E1; 16 mm from T1E2), and more powerful and reliable. By copying the Vickers six-tonner, Ordnance was on schedule to deliver something to rival the Soviet T26, the best light of the period.

However, Ordnance became increasingly deferential to the two users. The infantry wanted mobile support from machine-guns and short howitzers, while the cavalry wanted faster. The T1E6 (December 1932) was the last in the T1 Light series. The infantry were left with the M1917, which gained a larger-engined variant (M1917A1) in 1929. As Graph 3 shows, the relative effectiveness of American tanks was falling, while their efficiency was rising (see Graph 4), given trends to lightness and longer operating range.

In 1934, the Ordnance Department started to try its T2 series, whose variants would be acquired by both the infantry (as light tanks) and the cavalry (as combat cars). Peacetime deliveries mounted only machine-guns and armor no thicker than on the T1 series, until the M2A3 Light of 1938 (22 mm). With increasing power, they achieved increasing speed, but the choice for radial engines and volute suspension made the tanks taller and less mobile across country than their peers.

All US tanks available at the start of the Second World War were light, except some stored Mark VIII Heavy Tanks. None was deployed in the Second World War, although wartime descendants were (M2A4, M3-M3A3, M5-M5A1, M8-M8A1).

The M1921 is photographed in May 1922 at the Aberdeen Proving Grounds.

Medium tanks

After the war, the British sent designs for the British medium tanks (Marks A through D), which influenced the first publicly-designed American medium tanks (M1921; M1922; T1 Medium of 1925). An officer with the infantry's tanks wrote: "England, with her modern equipment, is far in advance of practically all other nations in tank development" (Icks 1929). The Chief of Ordnance reported that "We are nothing like so far advanced in the matter of tanks as the British; they have been at it longer, spent more money and made more progress than anybody else. No other country has developed tanks of such range and speed." (in: Peck 1946: 395)

Almost all the Christie tanks were tried by the Ordnance Department on behalf of the cavalry, which encouraged faster, lighter versions, until Christie was offering turret-less chassis in the light class – so highly tuned that only his driver could make them work. In 1922 he offered the M1921, which was effectively his M1919 with the armament moved to the nose. He chose the same configuration for the M1928. The M1930 was essentially the M1928 with space for a turret, which needed

A M1931, confusingly known also as M1930, with one-man turret, short 37-mm gun, and convertibility to running without tracks.

Ordnance officials test a T3E2 in 1934. This featured a two-man turret, four machine-guns, a more reliable engine, and no convertibility.

to be developed by its Soviet, Polish, and British recipients. From 1931, Ordnance tried his M1931 tank (essentially a M1930 with a turret). Dissatisfied with Christie's responsiveness, Ordnance developed its own version (T3E2), which was certainly the most viable American version of a Christie platform, but still inferior to foreign developments from the same chassis. Ordnance persisted with a minor evolution (T3E3), while Christie went his own way, developing a smaller turretless vehicle, to be delivered to the battlefield by air with detachable wings.

America in the 1930s looks like Britain in the 1920s: diverse suppliers were piloting innovative tanks, whose effectiveness was high and rising, relative to most countries (see Graph 5), but the Army was standardizing the cheapest and lightest.

The cavaly was satisfied with light tanks. The infantry was satisfied but mindful of foreign re-investment in mediums. In 1938, Rock Island Arsenal derived from the M2 Light platform the M2 Medium, which, in June 1939, became the first medium to be standardized for use by the US Army. (Mass production started in August.) The M2 Medium barely differentiated from the lights. Thus, few were produced, and none was deployed, while a much larger version was developed (M3 Medium). The latter was not ready until 1941, and regrettably adopted the French heavy tank configuration, with main armament in the hull (see Volume II).

American realization

US official historians admitted that the US Army was unready for World War II by every measure of tank warfare (quantity, qualities, structure, doctrine). All US tanks and most other vehicles deployed during wartime were developed during wartime, despite the fact that the US Army tried or piloted about as many types from 1919 to 1939 as the French and Soviets. The US did not standardize a heavy tank until 1945. By contrast, most US firearms started production during neutrality, and remained in front-line use throughout the war (US ASF 1948: 3-4).

An American analyst found that US tanks were inferior despite "the most

This M2A1 Medium was delivered in 1940, with slightly thicker armor, wider tracks, and uprated engine over the M2. In the background is a M3 light, with M3A1 turret, of late 1942. This photograph was taken at Aberdeen in 2005, before the tanks were moved to other collections.

advanced automotive and tractor industry in the world, matched by a trained, educated work force." American "tank designers were constrained to take advantage of advancing civilian technology" by their sensitivity to rapid obsolescence and unreliable funding (Alexander 1976: 4-5, 17-25).

A separate analyst agreed that the tanks available to the US Army at the start of the Second World War were obsolete. "[T]he US Army mustered only a few light tanks from the last war, although the United States was the world leader in automotive development," as proven later by "the Jeep, cargo and troop trucks, and earth-moving equipment." (Jones 1999: 215)

Chrysler was one of America's five top automobile producers, but uninvolved in tanks until the war. The company acknowledged that Europeans led in tank technology, even though Americans boasted the largest automotive industry. Chrysler took comfort in its claim to catch-up during wartime. "It is in the practical application of such discoveries that we [Americans] are supreme." (Stout 1946: 76)

Nevertheless, peacetime legacies cursed most of America's wartime tanks. Evolutions from the peacetime light tank series were not broken by a revolutionary platform until late 1944 (M24, Chaffee). The M3 Medium served into 1943 with the US Army, and through 1945 with Allied armies. The main medium in Western service was a variant with the main armament in the turret (M4 Medium). Legacy radial engines and volute suspension contributed to make this taller, less mobile across country, and less easy to upgrade than peer mediums (the Soviet T34 and German Panzer IV). No revolutionary medium design was deployed by US forces until early 1945 (M26, Pershing), which was later reclassified as heavy (see Volume II).

CHAPTER 7

Italian and Japanese exceptionalism

Italy and Japan, despite mobilizing for war in the 1930s, still ended the decade with surprisingly small and light tank forces. They were too remote to influence each other, but they shared Western influences. They fought on the Western Allied side during the First World War, and shared access to French and British exports, although initially they chose heavier requirements. They became antagonistic towards their former allies by the 1930s, but curiously adopted Western trends to lighter tanks. Their similar geopolitics are partial explanations: long coastlines and mountainous interiors at home; under-developed, close terrain in colonies overseas. In both states, the navy was the strongest service, followed by the air force. Their armies acquired excellent off-road wheeled vehicles, but their tanks fell behind.

Italian tankettes

In one way, Italy is the most disappointing of the interwar developers. It had been first to develop a turreted heavy tank, and to copy the FT light, but for most of the peace it foolishly issued only tankettes.

In 1929, the Italians acquired 21 Carden-Loyd Mark VI machine-gun carriers of the latest design, with overhead cover. The Italians classified the type as "fast tank" (*Carro Veloce*) and designated it, after the year of acquisition, as the CV29. An Italian joint venture with Vickers (*Odero Terni Orlando*; OTO) produced four copies, each armed with a 6.5-mm machine-gun by Fiat. From this type, Ansaldo (a state-owned steel works) evolved a close derivative, with automotive components by Fiat, and 12-mm instead of 9-mm armor. This was piloted in 1931, further developed in 1932, and procured in 1933 as the CV33. In 1934, a new version (CV35) was developed,

The Carden-Loyd Mark VI of 1929, with overhead protection for the crewmen.

A CV35, still in use in 1943.

with twin Fiat M1935 8-mm machine-guns, a modified casemate, modified vision ports and slits, modified suspension, armor up to 14-mm thick, and bolts in place of some rivets. Subsequent modifications (twin Breda M1938 machine-guns, torsion bar suspension, stowage bin on top of track guards) were collected as a new model in 1938. In the same year, the CVs were reclassified as light tanks, and designated L3s, so the three platforms became L3/33, L3/35, and L3/38 (Cappellano and Battistelli 2012a: 14-15, 40).

In 1935, Ansaldo piloted two one-man tankettes, one with twin 6.5-mm guns (*Mitragliatrice d'Assalto*), the other with a 45-mm mortar (*Moto-mortaio blindato d'Assalto*). The superstructure consisted of a 14-mm shield at the front, and thinner plates on the side, but no roof or rear plate. The whole vehicle was 3.6 feet (1.1 m) tall. Despite a low weight of 470 kilos (1,036 pounds), it reached only 5 kph (3.1 mph), given an engine developing just 5 metric hp. Fortunately, this death trap never entered service (Cappellano and Battistelli 2012a: 18).

Italian light tanks

The Army's requirement was focused on supporting the infantry in the assault, but its specifications vacillated between tankettes and self-propelled guns. By 1934, it was sponsoring turreted light tanks, but did not get one in mass production until 1941, with technologies that hardly improved on legacies. In 1935, Ansaldo delivered its first turreted tank, based on a CV35. The turret mounted a 37mm L26 gun and coaxial machine-gun, with another machine-gun on the turret as an anti-aircraft weapon. In theory, this was superior to British lights, but the Italian Army rejected it, and its anti-

An L6/40, as delivered in 1941.

Ansaldo's 10-tonner and 8-tonner, in 1938.

aircraft version (with twin machine-guns), given a high center of gravity. The next version (1936) had the main armament in the hull, and two machine-guns in a small turret, but was rejected for insufficient ammunition. The third version (1937) had no turret. The Army ordered 200 vehicles, but cancelled them given dissatisfactory trials of the pilot.

The Army's lack of clarity and urgency seems more curious given concurrent operational disappointments with tankettes. Truck-borne tankettes fulfilled rare requirements in poorly developed mountainous terrain at home and in colonies, but proved insufficiently mobile and survivable in Ethiopia in 1935, and useless against real tanks in Spain from 1936.

The Army had specified the first light at 5 tons. In 1938, it specified a 7-ton tank, with a turret armed with either twin 8-mm machine-guns or a 20-mm gun with coaxial machine-gun. The first version included an option on a flamethrower in the hull. Ansaldo submitted a 6-ton pilot in October 1939, with twin machine-guns. In 1940, it tried a larger version, with a 37 L26 gun and coaxial machine-gun, followed by a variant with a 20mm L65 cannon and coaxial machine-gun. The latter was accepted as the L6/40, although deliveries did not start until May 1941.

Italian mediums

Beside the Carden-Loyd carriers, Italy acquired a Vickers Mark E ("six-tonner") Type A (twin turrets). While the USSR was developing this into the excellent T26 tank, Ansaldo, with automotive parts from Fiat, developed a self-propelled 65-mm howitzer, classified as "breakthrough tank" (*Carro di Rottura*), despite no turret. In Italian marketing material and British intelligence, the vehicle was known as an 8-tonner, even though it was specified at 9 metric tons.

Liddell Hart enjoyed privileged access. In late 1931, he wrote that some Carden-Loyd carriers and a Vickers six-tonner were being tried, and "an eight-ton Ansaldo has been designed" (1932c: 286). Ansaldo delivered the latter in early 1932.

Each of the Italian tankettes and light tanks accommodated just two men. In 1936, the Army specified a three-man 10-ton tank, which would eventually spawn Italy's first medium (M11/39). However, it was given the current 5-tonner's hybrid tank/assault gun configuration (main armament in the hull; twin 8-mm machine-guns in the turret). Its two differentiations from the 9-ton offering were: longer main armament (37-mm L40); and 30-mm armor (although the L6 would soon be specified with 40 mm). The first pilot was delivered in 1937, with running gear adapted from the L3/35 tankette. The second pilot (May 1938) was developed from the 9-ton chassis, with new superstructure, turret, and engine. This "10-ton tank"

Experimental Tank Number 1, in 1927

was standardized as the M11/39 ("11" for its true weight, "39" for its year of mass production). By then a 13-ton replacement (M13) was in development, with 47-mm gun and 40-mm armor, but would not be standardized until 1940. Thus, as Graphs 5 and 6 show, both effectiveness and efficiency fell furthest in Italy.

The peacetime Army was curiously unhurried, unambitious, and uninspired. No source gives an adequate explanation. Patrick Wright judged that Italy lacked industrial capacity for a peer mechanized army, "aggravated by Mussolini's policy of national economic independence or 'autarchy,' and insufficiently alleviated by his late announcement, in February 1939, of a policy intended to 'motorize the nation'" (2000: 210). However, Italy had capacity for better, as proven by its excellent armored cars and off-road logistical vehicles. The industrial problem was that the Army acquiesced in a duopoly (Fiat and Ansaldo), which effectively cooperated as a monopoly. The Army was at fault for confused and unambitious requirements. At root was Liddell Hart's promise of cheap, swarming tankettes, which influenced the excessive light-weight and hull-mountings of the turreted lights and mediums.

Japanese medium tanks

In 1922, Japan acquired several FT tanks with 37 mm guns. These were still in service in 1940 (Roland 1975: 6). Already, the infantry (the user arm) was ambitious for heavier. In 1925, it required 10-ton and 20-ton tanks (respectively 11 and 22 US tons). At Japan's instigation, Vickers developed a tank for the light requirement, although this would weigh closer to 12 tons and be designated by Vickers as the Medium C (not to be confused with the earlier Medium C by Foster and TD&E). Meanwhile, the Japanese developed the 20-ton requirement indigenously, albeit in cooperation with Vickers. The product would weigh about 18 metric tons (19.8 US). The two vehicles were only six tons apart, the difference attributable mostly to armor (6.5 mm on the Medium C, up to 17 mm on the other) and crewmen (four in the Medium C, five in the other). They were similar in armament: each boasted a 57-mm gun in the main turret, a machine-gun in a separate mounting in the front, and a machine-gun in a turret towards the rear. The Medium C had an additional machine-gun in each side of the hull, like the Vickers Light/Medium.

The indigenous design was tried first, in February 1927, as Experimental Tank Number 1 (known as Type 87 in the West). Development continued to the Type 91, tried in 1932, with slightly thicker armor (20 mm), and more power and speed. This was developed into the Type 95 (tried in 1934), with a short 70-mm gun as main

戦車の勇姿
A Type 89, as mass produced from 1931 to 1934, with a vertical plate in front of the driver and (on his right) the machine-gunner.

armament, a short 37-mm gun in a forward turret, and armor up to 35 mm thick. Weight reached 26 metric tons (25.6 long; 28.7 US), which was classified as heavy at the time, but clearly medium by the 1940s.

In March 1927, the Japanese received the Medium C. British officials (having inspected it in January) admitted this was superior to the Vickers Light/Medium, except in survivability. The Medium C had a larger engine, larger turret, larger gun, and longer, taller running gear (for lower ground pressure and better obstacle-crossing) (Tank & Tracked Transport Technical Sub-Committee, Minute 70, 29th

Type 89Bs in the Philippines in 1942. This type had a single plate in front, reversed the driver and machine-gunner positions, and received a more powerful diesel engine.

Type 97 (Chi-Ha) tanks of the first model, with added frame aerials.

March 1927, RACTM E2010.301). One peculiarity was that all three fuel tanks were mounted on the trackguards. At the first Japanese trial, the vehicle failed to take an incline, the engine backfired, the petrol ignited, and two engineers from Vickers were injured in fighting the fire. Four months later a replacement engine arrived.

Within two years, the Japanese tried their own copy, initially classed as a light, later as a medium (Type 89, Yi-Go or Chi-Ro). This had the same armament and armor as the Experimental Tank Number 1, with slightly better mobility. It was slightly shorter and lighter than the Medium C, thanks to a smaller engine (by Daimler of Germany) and deletion of the two side machine-guns. The type served operationally from 1932 throughout the war, albeit relegated from 1938 behind the unrelated Type 97 (Roland 1975: 8-15).

The Type 97 (Chi-ha) offered a much lower profile and thicker armor (25 mm). A more powerful engine, larger wheels, and improved suspension enabled increased speed (38 kmh; 24 mph). Although heavier (15.2 metric tons) than the Type 89, it was still lighter than most foreign medium tanks. For its weight, it was an excellent platform. It just needed a better anti-tank weapon, which started development in 1939. Service and development continued throughout the war.

Japanese light tanks

Japan's trend to light tanks was curiously late but strong. Other than imported FTs, they date to 1929, when the cavalry required them in addition to armored cars. Given the infantry's control of tanks, the cavalry classified them as Heavy Armored Cars. Appropriately, they were known as Cavalry Tanks too, although Western intelligence, and thence historians, called them tankettes. The inspiration was the Carden-Loyd Mark VI carrier, but Japan jumped straight to turreted derivatives.

In 1932, a pilot was demonstrated, with a 6.5-mm machine-gun in the turret, another in the front hull, three crewmen, and a weight around 3.5 metric tons (3.9 US), with 6-mm armor. The mass product (1933) featured 12-mm armor. This was designated Type 92 Heavy Armored Car (misidentified as Type 93 Tankette in the

West). By 1937, a new version was delivered, with four larger wheels each side (in place of six small wheels) and a 13-mm machine gun in the front hull. The last version (1941) had 7.7-mm instead of 6.5-mm guns.

From 1934, production of Type 92 Heavy Armored Cars was surpassed by a two-man tank, without the hull machine-gun (Type 94 Light Armored Car; misidentified as Type 92 Tankette in the West). This was developed with a short 37-mm gun, and 16-mm armor, still with two crewmen, and a weight under 5 tons (Type 97, Te-Ke; piloted in November 1937, produced from 1939).

A Type 92 Heavy Armored Car of the first design.

By 1935, each division required a company of five cavalry tanks, but, overall, the cavalry's requirement was not great. The infantry concurrently drove a much larger requirement for light tanks. In 1933, it required a three-man, 7.5-ton tank that would be easier to transport and sustain than the mediums. In 1934, it tried a pilot Type 95 (Ha-Go), then sent it for field trials in Manchuria, before ordering final development in 1935. The Type 95 was armed with a 37-mm gun in the turret, one 6.5 mm machine in the front hull, another in the turret rear. It was armored up to 16 mm. Although only about 1,000 were produced from 1936 to 1943, it was the most numerous type in Imperial Japan's service, given that Japan produced only 2,515

A Type 92 Heavy Armored Car with new running gear, a 13-mm machine-gun in the front, and 7.7-mm machine-guns in and on the turret.

Type 34 Light Armored Cars of the first type, being serviced.

tanks from 1939 to 1945 (Ellis, 1990; Ellis, 1993; Ness, 2002).

Overall, as Graph 5 shows, the effectiveness of Japan's tanks was relatively low, although higher than Italy's, and trending slightly up. As Graph 6 shows, efficiency trended towards second best, as appropriate during imperial, but not world, wars.

A Type 95 (Ha-Go) at Fort DeRussy, Hawaii.

CHAPTER 8

Soviet, German, and Czech catch-up

Once Western forces departed Russia (1920), the Bosheviks consolidated their empire (1922), and Josef Stalin consolidated his rule (1924). Western insight practically disappeared for more than a decade. In that time, Western forces did not foresee the USSR jumping ahead: they had departed an enormous agricultural state; they knew the early industrial boasts were exaggerated; and they heard of famines and purges. Yet Western forces had left their best light, medium, and heavy tank types with White Russian forces, which the Bolsheviks captured. Additionally, German forces asked for Soviet cooperation in 1919, as they departed the Eastern European territories that they had occupied since 1917.

A secret organization (*Sondergruppe R*) coordinated arms production in Russia from 1921 to 1933. Further agreements (July 1922; March 1926) traded military products and services for Soviet facilities. In 1923, the German Army established a headquarters in Moscow, to set up training and testing bases elsewhere in Russia, of which the fourth and final was for tanks (at Kazan, on the upper Volga, in 1929) (Speidel 1949: 24-25, 57-59, 76-77, 102). In 1930, the Soviets withdrew from cooperative training, to focus on German technology. From 1927 to 1933, the Soviets had sole foreign access to German tank trials, except in Sweden and Germany. They accessed equipment at the border during import. They examined more equipment inside Germany, at German invitation (Speidel 1949: 16-18, 21, 44, 120-128). The Nazi regime (elected in January 1933) withdrew this cooperation, but the Soviets had spies inside the economics ministry and the Army weapons office.

Nazi Panzers trended lighter, but nonetheless culminated, in peacetime, in the Panzer IV: the only peacetime platform to stay in production through World War II. Meanwhile, Germany made up its numbers with excellent Czechoslovakian tanks.

Soviet tanks

From the start, the Soviets aimed for industrialization to rival the West, and to steal, import, and copy technologies in pursuit of technological superiority too. Their first indigenous tank dates to 1920, when the Sormovo shipyard and locomotive factory (on the Volga, west of Kazan) refurbished 14 FT tanks, and assembled a single copy. Slowly, a new type was derived, with improved suspension (MS1, or T18, of 1928), followed by a medium-weight version (T12, of 1929) (see Graph 3).

Subsequent developments from imports were quicker and more impressive. In 1930, Vickers agreed to supply tankettes, amphibious light tanks, and fast light-medium tanks, and to allow Soviet engineers to participate in their assembly. The Soviets used a few imports of each design, assembled copies under license, and developed derivatives. The most consequential of the Vickers tanks was the Mark E or Six-Tonner, which the British Army never acquired but spawned a long Soviet series of light tanks (T26). The import had two turrets, each armed with a machine-gun. By 1931, the Soviets were producing copies, by 1932 a version with a short 37-mm gun in one of the turrets, by 1933 a version with a long 45-mm gun in a single turret. Production continued into 1941, after more than 10,000 vehicles.

A T26 on display in Spain, 1938.

In 1931, the Soviets imported a Christie M1930 tank, which they designated BT1. By October of the same year they piloted a copy with a 37-mm gun in a turret of their own design (BT2). This was five years before the British imported a M1930. The BT2 was mass-produced and issued from 1932, seven years before the British issued their derivative (Cruiser III). The BT5 (1933) carried a larger gun, better sloped armor, and a more powerful engine than the Cruiser III. The BT5 and T26 were certainly the best tanks of the Spanish War (1936-1939) and the USSR-Japan confrontations of the same era. More importantly, the BT series grew into the A32 pilots (1939) and thence the T34, which served from 1940 into the Cold War. The T34 and its upgrades were years ahead of concurrent British Cruisers.

The Red Army tried fewer types than the US and French armies from 1919 to 1939, but the most types in the 1930s, when they trended most effective (see Graph 5) and efficient (see Graph 6). The Red Army deployed some monstrous follies, including the multi-turreted 28-ton T28 of 1933, 54-ton T35 of 1934, 55-ton SMK of 1939, and 58-ton T100 of 1939, but its light (T26), light-medium (BT), medium (T34), and heavy (KV) series were the best of the period.

By 1935, Soviet superiority, in quantity and quality, was known in the West, although not well explained. For instance, Hobart (then acting as both commander of the Tank Brigade and Inspector of the RTC, wrote to the General Staff:

> At the present moment it would appear that only Russia is attempting to develop really modern equipment and a conscript army at the same time. Russia, being the most autocratic of powers, is able to retain personnel which she requires to handle technical equipment for as many years as she thinks desirable. It remains to be seen however, whether such a system can be made efficient; it certainly involves an enormous effort in men and money. (IRTC to DSD, 22nd March 1935, LHCMA Lindsay)

The BT5 was developed in 1933, with the same 45-mm gun as the T26 M1933. This turret has a frame aerial.

A post-war American think-tank found that the USSR leveraged imports and second-mover advantages to innovate in ways the US would not match until the late 1940s (Alexander 1976: 4, 17-25). This was a minor study without commercial release. Few commercial publications compared and contrasted Soviet and Western tank developments, although the experts realized that the Soviets developed better tanks in the 1930s despite less industrial capacity (Simpkin 1987: 169). By contrast, an academic historical study of "military effectiveness," sponsored by the US government, claimed that the Soviets between the world wars proved the "rule [that] more advanced forces generally rely on internal sources of supply" and that imported tanks tend to be inferior (Millett, Murray, and Watman 1988: 5).

T35 Heavies parade in Red Square, circa 1937, with a 76-mm gun in the top turret, a 45-mm gun in the front and rear main turrts, and machine-guns elsewhere.

Rheinmetall's Grosstraktor was the only variant with side doors. This photograph was taken in 1932, after modifications to the running gear.

German tanks

Westerners under-estimated German capacity for tank development. They dimissed the A7V as immobile, and paid even less attention to Germany's light, medium, and super-heavy developments of the Great War. Peacetime development seemed unlikely. Germany agreed at Versailles in 1919 to eschew tanks, heavy guns, war planes, and battleships, and to cede industry, money, and territory.

Secretly, the Germans kept a stake in Landsverk, and rotated some designers and requirers there. Landsverk focused on light tanks, which explains why, in 1925, the Army's Weapons Office specified a medium tank (15-16 metric tons) for home development. This was meant to be amphibious, perhaps inspired by the TD&E's trials of an amphibious Heavy Mark IX and its own Light Supply Carrier, Light Infantry Tank, and Tropical Tank. These were propelled by tracks, and (except the latter) lacked turrets. The Germans specified a propeller and turrets. The configuration was similar to the first Japanese mediums, whose specifications were agreed in the same year, and possibly leaked from Vickers. The Germans chose a 75-mm gun in a forward turret, and a machine-gun in a rear turret (with high elevation for anti-aircraft use), without the side guns of the Vickers Medium C.

Krupp was contracted to work on the turrets. In 1926, each of Krupp, Daimler-Benz (which had assembled A7Vs), and Rheinmetall was contracted to design, develop, and deliver two tanks. These were despatched to Kazan in 1929 (with the cover name of *Grosstraktor*). Each carried the same turret, although Krupp modified the mountings on its own vehicles. Daimler's running gear was suspended on leaf springs (and would prove slowest and least reliable), Rheinmetall's by hydraulic pistons (replaced by coils later), and Krupp's by coils (which proved slightly faster but not quite as reliable). All were repeatedly modified in Russia until return in 1933. Some joined manoeuvres in 1935, before retirement as gate guardians.

By 1928, Krupp was ordered to design, develop, and deliver a 6-ton light tank (coded as *Kleinetraktor*, later *Leichttraktor*). In 1929, Rheinmetall and Daimler were invited to do the same, although Daimler soon reduced its responsibilities to the engine only. Krupp designed a common turret, although Rheinmetall assembled it. The armament was specified initially as the 75-mm L24 (as developed for the *Grosstraktor*), later as a 37-mm L45. Both offered more capacity than the 47-mm in

Krupp's Leichttraktor, as delivered in May 1930.

the Vickers Light/Medium. Krupp and Rheinmetall each delivered two vehicles in May 1930. They entrained for Kazan in the same month. Krupp's offering proved inferior, due to a single leaf spring suspending each running gear. The Rheinmetall had three bogies each side, each suspended by a leaf spring, although this also needed modification. In 1932, they were returned for trials of coil suspension.

In that year, Daimler-Benz, Krupp, Rheinmetall, Henschel, and Maschinenfabrik Augsburg Aktiengesellschaft (MAN) were asked to bid on a less ambitious project. Krupp got a jump start by importing from the USSR two Carden-Lloyd Mark VI carriers (which the Soviets had received from Vickers). In 1933, Krupp delivered derivatives (coded *Kleinetraktors*, later *Krupptraktors*). In 1934, Krupp's platform was combined with Daimler-Benz's turret to create the Panzer I (Jentz 1996: I, 8–10).

Also in 1932, the Army required a more lethal and survivable development of the *Grosstraktor*. The National Socialist Party, elected in January 1933, made this urgent. Adolf Hitler opposed Soviet socialism and interference in Eastern Europe,

A Panzer 1A, as produced from 1934 to 1936. The Panzer 1B had a larger engine, an extended rear, and a raised idler.

In February 1939, a *Neubaufahrzeug VI* is displayed at the Berlin Motor Show, alongside a Panzer II.

and wanted to be self-reliant. He withdrew Germany's military missions that year.

Rheinmetall was made lead contractor, given preference for its version of the *Grosstraktor*. The new tank was disguised as *Mittleretraktor* and, later, "new-built vehicle" (*Neubaufahrzeug*). Two mild steel pilots were delivered in 1934. At least one was fitted with a mounting to Rheinmetall's design, with a 37-mm L45 above a 75-mm L24 (*Neubaufahrzeug V*). Krupp made them coaxial (*Neubaufahrzeug VI*). On the right of the mantlet was a ball-mounted machine-gun. A smaller turret forward, and another rearward, were armed with a machine-gun. Krupp assembled three armour steel tanks from 1935 to 1936, which would be used in Norway in 1940.

The *Neubaufahrzeug* looked like the Vickers Medium Mark III of 1929, although British influence was more doctrinal than technological. Liddell Hart alleged that "the Germans certainly learnt…from the trials of our first Tank Brigade on Salisbury Plain in 1931, under [Charles] Broad, and then [from 1934] the more advanced exercises that were carried out by this brigade under [Percy] Hobart" (to Richard Ogorkiewicz, 16th August 1949, RACTM E2015.2015.58). Hobart remembered his overnight maneuvers of September 1934 as most formative:

> Foreign military attaches were very prominent at these maneuvers. Years afterwards the British military attaché in Berlin told me he had been able to see the report of the German military attaché on these maneuvers. This report had insisted strongly on the epoch-making nature of the maneuver he had seen and how it opened up a new era of warfare. He urged that Germany should develop tank forces at once on these lines. He also commented that fortunately the British military had failed to perceive the great possibilities of this idea and showed no signs of developing it. (to unknown addressee, 4th January 1942, RACTM E1968.30.5)

When Major-General James Marshall-Cornwall (an intelligence and artillery officer) visited Berlin in March 1935, the Defence Minister (Field-Marshal Werner Blomberg) remarked that German handling of armored formations benefited from British writings. "This was cold comfort to me in view of the hesitating steps which the British Army was taking in that direction." (Marshall-Cornwall 1984: 97) In Autumn 1935, Fuller complained that "though the development of mechanisation in foreign armies has been and still is restricted by cost, 'tank mindedness' has been

After 35 Panzer 4As (1937-1938), the 4B (below) was introduced, with frontal armour doubled to 30-mm. Subsequent marks were rated for 300 metric hp, instead of 250.

developed out of all proportion when compared to our own." (Fuller 1936: 455)

Grosstraktor and *Neubaufahrzeug* were revealed in the maneuvers of Summer 1935 (after Hitler publicly revealed rearmament in March). Westerners were alarmed by the great number of Panzer Is displayed at this time, but could take comfort that the Germans genuinely thought of it as a training vehicle. On the other hand, most British and US tanks were lights with no better armament.

They were not to know that in 1934 the Germans initiated projects that would produce Panzer II (1936), Panzer III (1937), and Panzer IV (1937). These were not as well armed, armored, or engined as Soviet peers, but featured superior ergonomics, communications, and optics. Their inferiorities were not the fault of the General Staff, whose Chief (1935-1938), General Ludwig Beck, wanted to match the French heavies. However, the Weapons Office prioritized production, partly given political pressure, partly out of conviction that quantity could swamp quality (Jentz 1996: I, 30-47). While the Panzers II to IV were less lethal and survivable than the French heavies and mediums, they outmatched the French, British, and US lights that proliferated in the same period. As Graph 5 shows, German tank effectiveness overtook the French in 1936. The overall effectiveness of British and American pilots stayed ahead, but the British and Americans were mass-producing few of them. Most importantly, the Panzers were easier to upgrade, such that the Panzer IV stayed in production from 1937 to 1945. No Western tank stayed in production longer than 1940 to 1944 (Valentine; variants were produced until 1945).

Moreover, the Germans got to the best platform in the West despite piloting fewer types between the world wars than each of France, Britain, and the US: just 19 types, on 7 platforms. Nineteen is fewer than Czechoslovakia piloted.

Czechoslovakian tanks

Czechoslovakia was one of the new states confirmed in 1919, from territories of the former German and Austro-Hungarian empires. It inherited fine automotive firms – including Tatra and Laurin & Klement; arms suppliers – such as Skoda; and engineering firms – such as Breitfeld-Danek. In 1923, the Army imported a few tracked agricultural tractors from Hanomag of Germany. At the same time, it bought from Joseph Vollmer (who had been principal designer of the German tanks of the Great War) a design for attaching pneumatic wheels on the outside of tracked running gear for lowering to the ground for travel by road. The Army ordered Breitfeld-Danek to develop from these designs a gun tractor (KH50: where *KH* is short for *Kolohousenka*, meaning "wheel-track," and 50 is the engine's horsepower). Two vehicles were delivered in 1924, of which one was armored and fitted with a turret (top right). This was Czechoslovakia's first tank – a two-man light tank with good armament (37-mm gun), armor (14 mm) and speed (15 kmh or 9 mph on tracks, 35 kmh or 22 mph on wheels). In 1927, Breitfeld-Danek merged with an unrelated engineering firm to form ČKD (Českomoravská Kolben-Daněk), which immediately diversified into cars, particularly after acquiring Praga of Prague. ČKD offered more powerful versions (KH60 in 1927; KH70 in 1929). Each was armed with a machine-gun, but "male" versions (with 37-mm gun) were planned. All were rejected.

In 1930, ČKD (really Praga) acquired 3 Carden-Loyd carriers and a license to assemble copies (CLP or P-I). By 1933, it developed a two-man tankette (*Tančík vz. 33*; Tankette Model 33) (second from top right), distinguished by a fully armored cab and a second machine-gun (fixed, operated by the driver). From this platform, ČKD developed a light

tank (*Lehký tank*; LT) of the same weight as the KH series (7.5 tons), with slightly thicker armor (15 mm). The turret of the pilot (P-II, of 1932) was armed with a 47-mm gun, the pre-production LT34 (1934) with a machine-gun, and the full production LT34 (1935) with a 37-mm gun (third from top).

Skoda of Pilsen acquired Laurin & Klement in 1925, then offered armored cars, followed by tracked vehicles, based on Carden-Loyd Mark VI carriers. The first Skoda tank (MU2, of 1931) used essentially the same chassis, with a small turret for the machine-gunner, a proud boxy tower for the driver, and an armored deck. However, armor was just 5.5 mm thick to compensate for the extra structures. Skoda's three-man two-machine-gun tankette (MU4, of 1932) also was rejected.

By 1935, both ČKD and Skoda were competing for the cavalry's requirement for a light tank, which Skoda won. The LT35 (production actually started in 1936) was well-armed for its time with a 37-mm gun and two machine-guns. It was also reasonably armored (25 mm) for its weight (10.5 tons). For the class, its engine was

A LT35, circa 1938.

powerful (125 hp, or, later, with twin carburetors, 150 hp). The vehicle was fast (25 mph), although unreliable, including in its pneumatic transmission and steering.

ČKD and Skoda started to cooperate on many close variants, marketed as light cavalry and infantry support tanks. They also developed mediums, at less than 17 tons, and, in 1937, a nominal heavy, at less than 19 tons. Most consequentially, ČKD developed the LT34 into what would be exported mainly as TNH but ordered by the Czechoslovakian Army as LT38 (for production in 1939). This boasted superior protection, transmission, and running gear (four large roadwheels each side, each pair suspended by semi-elliptic leaf springs). Thanks to more efficient architecture, it was slightly lighter than the LT35. It has been described as "roughly equal to the Panzer III in strength and utility" (Mitcham 2007: 14).

The LT35 and LT38 were well armed, armored, and mobile for their weight, made more remarkable by the fact that their suppliers were innovating without much foreign cooperation. By 1937, Czechoslovakian tank effectiveness trended second to Soviet (see Graph 5). The main beneficiary was Germany, which occupied the country from October 1938 to March 1939. The German Army took the LT35 into service as the Panzer 35(t) ("t" abbreviates the German word for "Czechoslovakian"). Germany ordered production of the LT38 as the Panzer 38(t), starting in 1939. Although the tank was relegated in 1942, variants stayed in production throughout the war.

A Panzer 38(t) at TankFest 2015.

Country	1916-1919			1920-1929			1930-1939			1916-1939		
	Pilots	Effe.	Effi.	Pilots	Effe.	Effi.	Pilots	Effe.	Effi.	Pilots	Effe.	Effi.
Britain	26	0.33	0.41	21	0.41	0.50	33	0.40	0.44	80	0.33	0.41
France	5	0.33	0.42	15	0.49	0.47	24	0.40	0.43	44	0.35	0.42
USA	8	0.32	0.40	9	0.45	0.47	24	0.41	0.45	41	0.36	0.43
Italy	1	0.30	0.36	3	0.47	0.53	12	0.38	0.43	16	0.35	0.42
Japan	-	-	-	2	0.37	0.47	11	0.37	0.44	13	0.34	0.43
USSR	-	-	-	3	0.41	0.46	28	0.45	0.47	31	0.39	0.47
Germany	6	0.35	0.38	3	0.56	0.55	16	0.40	0.44	25	0.35	0.41
Czechoslovakia	-	-	-	3	0.37	0.49	17	0.42	0.45	20	0.37	0.44
Total or average	46	0.33	0.39	59	0.44	0.49	165	0.40	0.44	270	0.35	0.43

Table 6: Pilot tank count, effectiveness, and efficiency, by nation and period.
Note: scores are relative to ideal type for each period, so should not be considered relative across periods.

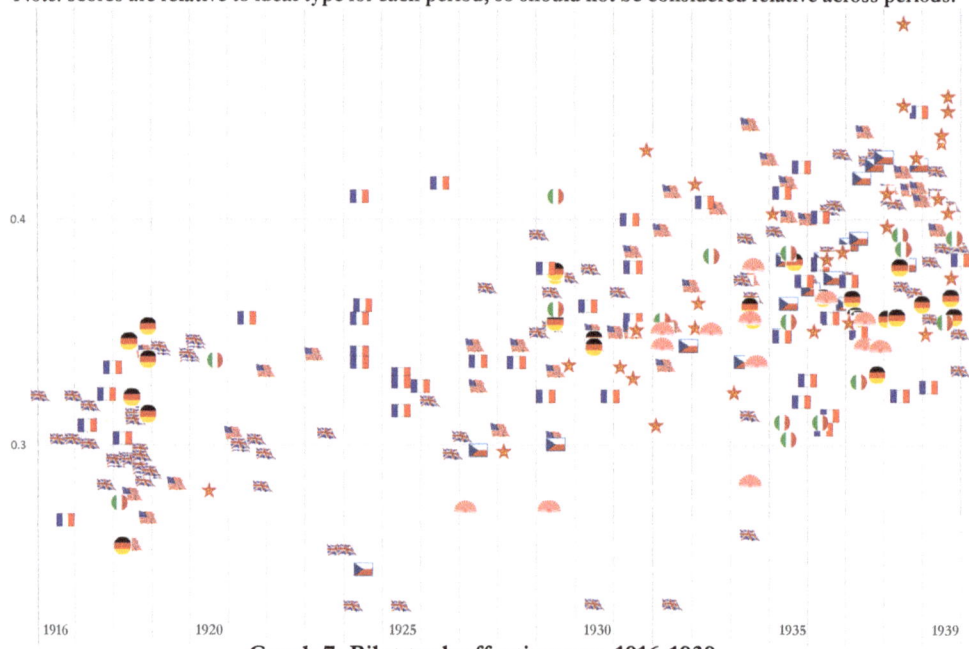

Graph 7: Pilot tank effectiveness, 1916-1939.

Graph 8: Pilot tank efficiency, 1916-1939

CHAPTER 9

Conclusion

During the First World War, the British deployed the first and best heavies and mediums, but the French deployed the first and best lights. The British heavies were the most mobile on the worst of battlefields. They were not as fast as mediums and lights, although in absolute terms the margins are small. Their inferiorities were in lethality and survivability. The Males mounted smaller capacity armaments than the French and German heavies. The Females carried fewer machine-guns than German heavies. The Germans deployed the best heavy on hard flat ground, and designed light, medium, and super-heavy tanks that would have shocked the Allies if war had continued into 1919. Italy built the first heavy with a turret. (The first tank produced with a turret was the FT.) The most disappointing designs were American: unambitious copies (e.g., M1917), improvisations (Holt gas-electric; Steam Tank), or tankettes (Ford). The one American design that rates well in the dataset was also the one most ignored (Skeleton tank) (see Graph 1).

The 1920s were a decade of extremes: the first-movers extended the effectiveness of their tanks (although Britain extended less than the others), while second-movers (USSR, Czechoslovakia, Japan) still ranked at the bottom (see Graph 7). Yet in the 1930s, Soviet and Czechoslovakian tanks averaged most effective. By incorporating Czechoslovakia, Germany joined the USSR in coming out of the interbellum best prepared for ground maneuver warfare, despite piloting no new types before 1929. The Soviets inherited no tank heritage except foreign tanks. Yet in the 1930s, Soviet tank effectiveness and efficiency led the world. By 1940 the Soviets had the best light (T26), light-medium (BT), medium (T34), and heavy (KV) series. How? Starting from scratch, they established heavy automotive factories, imported, stole, and reverse-engineered foreign technologies, and cooperated with Germany.

Weimar Germany was most internationally constrained. Nevertheless, its pilots of the 1920s were innovative, and certainly more lethal than Western competitors. Ultimately they benefited the USSR most. Nazi Germany rushed to catch up. It acquired mostly Panzer Is, which were less ambitious than any prior German type. Tellingly, that platform was based on the least impressive British export (a carrier). Nevertheless, within a few years, Germany got to the Panzer IV, armed with the same gun as developed for the *Grosstraktor* in the 1920s, with capacity for guns and armor sufficient to keep it in production and service through World War II.

The German Army developed astute requirements, partly by studying World War I, partly by observing foreign experiments, partly by experimenting in Sweden and Russia. At home, it developed new suppliers from 1925, something the British would not do until 1936. Moreover, it invited both co-development and competitive bids, combining public specialization with commercial competition. It invited three bidders on the *Grosstraktor*. By Panzer I, the number had grown to five.

While Western procurers usually contracted one design authority and parent assembler, the Germans increasingly combined major sub-assemblies (engine, transmission, turret, gun, superstructure, chassis) from different bidders (Wright 2000: 220). Inexperienced suppliers matured quicker in Germany thanks to longer apprenticeships and shorter periods of depreciation tax write-offs (enabling quicker acquisition of new tools) (Stout 1946: 76). Germany's enemies would claim they were outspent, but this was not true. In 1936, the Army lacked money to switch production to new types. In 1939, tanks accounted for 3% of army spending on new production (Jentz 1996: I, 34; Tooze 2006: 211, 371).

Although the Panzer IV was a fine platform, it arrived late, so German tank effectiveness for the 1930s as a whole ranks in the middle (see Graph 5). Germany's tank efficiency looks even worse (see Graph 6). Continental war arrived in 1939, quicker than the regime planned. German belligerency was enabled by Czechoslovakian tanks, whose effectiveness was second to only the Soviets. From 1938 to 1939, Germany acquired enough Panzer 35(t) and Panzer 38(t) tanks to make up 11 percent of the tank force that invaded Poland in September 1939.

The Czechoslovakians achieved their developmental successes after inheriting excellent automotive and arms capacities, licensing foreign technologies, and innovating at home, in a reasonably competitive marketplace. Their last and finest tank of the interbellum (LT38) was achieved with some cooperation across the two main competitors (CKD and Skoda), incentivized by strong export sales.

Italy and Japan sided with Germany in the 1930s, although this had no effect on peacetime tank development. Western trends were strong in both countries. Both relied on French FT tanks as their first tanks in service. Both took British imports as their inspiration in the 1920s. In Italy's case, the infantry encouraged tankettes and assault guns. Japan's cavalry belatedly pushed for light tanks, then the infantry jumped aboard. Italy's performance was worst, given reduction of a mature automotive sector to a duopoly (Ansaldo and Fiat) acting as a monopoly.

While Soviet and German public authorities developed new suppliers, Western equivalents tended to wait for private innovation. This error was compounded by distribution of requirements to both the infantry and cavalry. Even in Britain, despite a permanent tank arm, the cavalry gained inordinate influence, which helps to explain why the effectiveness of British tanks fell relatively, while their efficiency rose (see Graphs 7 and 8). The infantry too were responsible. Even when infantry-support requirements were filled by heavies (France from the 1920s) or mediums (Britain in late 1930s), they proved under-weight during World War II.

Britain and America started and ended the interbellum with public leadership of tank design and development. In between, from the mid-1920s to mid-1930s, they relied on the private sector to innovate for itself, and on the infantry and cavalry arms to determine requirements. This resulted in consolidation and regression, from which they were only just escaping in the late 1930s. By then, US, British, and French public authorities were taking over, but the rush to expand production resulted in a proliferation of proprietary types, technologies, and supply chains.

Britain fell furthest. The War Office exited the First World War with design authority over the best heavy and medium tanks, thanks to public sponsorship and co-development. The Superintendent of Design developed the best light to medium tractors, carriers, and tanks, and co-operated with Vickers in the best heavy tank of the 1920s (the Independent). However, the Ministry of Munitions allowed its TD&E to act independently of user specifications, producing more mobile but less survivable and less lethal light and medium tanks. The WO's mistake, after inheriting the TD&E in 1921, was to let it expire in 1923, rather than reform it. Its further mistake was to under-invest in the Superintendent of Design, while investing in the Vickers Light/Medium Mark I (1923). Vickers consolidated a monopoly. From 1929, the

Army received only Vickers lights and mediums (including the A6s and Medium Mark IIIs), until 1936, when the Superintendent of Design's new section for tracked and fighting vehicles (DDM) developed new suppliers. Still, the WO was in a rush, still biased to light and cheap, and still torn between the infantry's requirement for support and the cavalry's requirement to pursue. It split medium requirements into two classes (infantry tank; cruiser), and split the cruisers into two sub-classes (light; heavy), and further split each of these by adding close-support variants.

The first two marks of cruiser were essentially light-mediums, designed, developed, and produced by Vickers. The superior cruiser line (from Cruiser III) was developed from an import (Christie M1930 hull) by DDM and a new contractor (Morris Motors, which later spun off its tank business as Nuffield Mechanisation).

The first infantry tank was a thickly armored two-man machine-gun platform by Vickers (Matilda I). The Matilda II was developed by DDM and a new contractor (Vulcan). This was the most survivable medium of the interbellum, and well armed, but slow. Poorly funded, its production was too little, too late. By the final years of the 1930s, Britain was in such a rush it acquired from Vickers a derivative of the Cruiser II as a stop-gap infantry tank (Valentine). At the same time, it contracted an inexperienced supplier for the Cruiser V, with a new supply chain (see Volume II).

France's infantry bias was reinforced in 1920, when the infantry took over the tank arm. This was still commanded by an artillery officer (Estienne), who chose to configure heavy and heavy-medium tanks with main armaments in the hull. The light/medium series (Char D) avoided this configuration, and was highly capable. However, by the 1930s, development was curbed by proliferation of lighter tanks.

One explanation is doctrinal. Macksey and Batchelor (1970: 59) were sure that French development peaked in the early 1930s, and was "inhibited by the insistence of her General Staff on tanks remaining tied to infantry pace…No matter how unimaginative French strategic and tactical employment of their tanks was to be, the creative imagination of their designers and engineers was of high quality."

Another explanation is the fortification of the border, which peaked in the later 1930s. It cost, by one estimate, the equivalent of 6,000 medium tanks (Fuller 1943: 98). Yet in the same period France found plenty of money for tanks, some of which were excellent (Mosier 2003: 53-54). By the time Germany invaded, France held around 5,900 tanks, about twice as many as Germany. It piloted the second most types in peacetime (after Britain), and accepted almost all into service. It ended up with a plethora of models that were either barely differentiated (lights and light-mediums) or over-optimized for narrow roles (heavies and super-heavies). Its medium tanks were excellent but under-resourced. French tanks were better armed and armored than most. However, they tended to be slower and badly configured. Most turrets accommodated just one man, acting as commander, gunner, loader, and (usually) signaller. The heavies mounted main armaments in the hull.

The explanation that is always neglected in the literature is the structure of the acquisitions system. France wasted its competitive industry by demanding the sharing of intellectual property. Then it allowed near monopolies in certain classes (most clearly: Renault in the light class), which tended to stagnate and insulate. In the mid-1930s it nationalized suppliers, and forced them to share technologies. However, those last developments were barely in production when Germany invaded in May 1940. That invasion succeeded within less than seven weeks, too quickly for France to bring its larger tank force and superior productivity to bear.

Could the West catch up in World War II? That is the subject of Volume II…

APPENDIX 1

DATASET METHODOLOGY

Tanks are complex systems of systems, with multiple capabilities and attributes that synergize and trade-off in ways that cannot be captured by a single figure of merit (such as gun size, weight, or speed). Tanks must be compared by many key capabilities and attributes, or not at all. Thus, I use indices (mathematical combinations) of variables in order to express each tank type's many attributes and capabilities as one cardinal number. By averaging across variables, these indices capture the key synergies and trade-offs. Each capability or attribute of each tank type is expressed as a proportion of the best available for the period (such as: 1916-1919; 1920s; 1930s; etc.). Thus, each tank type's score is relative to the period's ideal type, as if the ideal type could have the best of each attribute. (The score for this impossibly ideal type would be 1.)

The tank effectiveness index is an average of the lethality, survivability, and tactical mobility indices (described below). The tank efficiency index averages these three with the strategic mobility index too. In all cases, a larger number is better. The effectiveness index captures typical trade-offs between capabilities. For instance, a tank might have a heavy gun, at the expense of amor. Similarly, increasing the gun or the armor will lower the power-to-weight ratio, unless a more powerful engine is fitted. The efficiency index captures the balance or trade-off between fighting effectiveness and the burdens of operational sustainment. We would expect a more effective tank, with a larger gun, more armor, and a more powerful engine, to be heavier and shorter in operational range, and thus more burdensome to transport and sustain.

The lethality index averages three attributes: main armament caliber (a correlate of destructiveness); gun barrel volume or capacity (a correlate of penetrativeness); muzzle velocity (a correlate of accuracy). Larger calibers allow larger and heavier projectiles, all other things equal. More gun volume suggests more capacity for imparting energy by internal combustion behind the projectile. Higher muzzle velocity suggests flatter trajectories and quicker time to target.

The survivability index averages two measures: horizontal thickness of armor (the best correlate of material resistance to kinetic attack); and height (a correlate of stealthiness and hide-ability). Nominal thickness and slope of the armor are used to calculate horizontal thickness. Since less height is better, the tank's height-as-a-proportion-of-maximum is deducted from one. The thickness of armor is calculated at the turret front, which receives a disproportion of hits. Where the thickness varies (as in cast mantlets), an average is used across the front.

The tactical mobility index averages four measures: engine power-to-weight; speed; nominal ground pressure; and vertical step. The mean maximum pressure is a superior measure to nominal ground pressure, but the former is missing too much data. Given that lower ground pressures are better, each tank type's pressure-as-a-proportion-of-maximum is deducted from one.

The strategic mobility index averages two measures: weight; and operating range. Lower weight suggests easier portability. Longer operating range indicates less burden on refueling assets. In order to achieve the same direction (larger is better), the tank's weight-as-a-proportion-of-maximum is deducted from one (because lower weights suggest lower transportation burden).

Tanks must be tracked, armored, armed, and (from 1924) turreted (except Italy until 1940). All documented pilots are considered, whether acquired or not.

APPENDIX 2

DATASET SOURCES

US tanks: US Army Ground Forces Board No. 2, Development of Armored Vehicles, Volume 1, Tanks, 1 September 1947; R.P. Hunnicutt, Sherman: A History of the American Medium Tank, Novato, CA: Presidio, 1976; Pershing: A History of the Medium Tank T20 Series, Novato, CA: Presidio, 1988; Firepower: A History of the American Heavy Tank, Novato, CA: Presidio, 1988; Stuart: A History of the American Light Tank, Novato, CA: Presidio, 1992; Hofmann, George F., and Donn A. Starry, eds., Camp Colt to Desert Storm: The History of US Armored Forces, Lexington, KY: University Press of Kentucky, 1999; Rob Cogan, Curator of the National Armor and Cavalry Museum, Fort Benning, Georgia.

British and Canadian tanks: Superintendent Tank Design & Experiment, "Tanks: Description & Constructional Details," January 1925 in RACTM, Tanks World War 1, Box 1; War Office, "Instruction Book for the Tank, Infantry, Mark I," 7 June 1939 and 17 July 1940; Vulcan Foundry, "Infantry Tank Mark IIA* Specification," August 1940; DRAC3, "AFV Abridged Specifications," 23 December 1944; Fighting Vehicles Design Establishment, "FV Data Booklet Number 1," circa 1948; Duncan Crow, ed., British AFVs, 1919-1940, Windsor: Profile, 1970; Bruce Oliver Newsome, Valentine Infantry Tank, 1938-1945, New Vanguard 233, London: Osprey, 2016.

French tanks: Francois Vauvillier, The Encyclopedia of French Tanks and Armoured Fighting Vehicles, 1914-1940, Paris: Histoire & Collections, 2014.

Italian tanks: Filippo Cappellano and Pier Paolo Battistelli, Italian Light Tanks, 1919-1945, New Vanguard 191, Oxford: Osprey, 2012a; Filippo Cappellano and Pier Paolo Battistelli, Italian Medium Tanks, 1939-1945, New Vanguard 195, Oxford: Osprey, 2012b.

Japanese tanks: Hara, Tomio, Japanese Medium Tanks, AFV Weapons Profiles No. 49, Great Bookham, England: Profile Publications Limited, 1972; Hara, Tomio, Japanese Combat Cars, Light Tanks, and Tankettes, AFV Weapons Profile No. 54, Great Bookham, England: Profile Publications Limited, 1973; McLean, Donald B., Japanese Tanks, Tactics and Antitank Weapons, Wickenburg, Arizona: Normount Technical Publications, 1973; Roland, Paul M., Imperial Japanese Tanks, 1918-1945, Kings Langley, England: Bellona Publications, 1975; Tomczyk, Andrzej M., Japanese Armor, five volumes, Gdansk, Poland: AJ Press, 2002; Taki, founder of http://www3.plala.or.jp/takihome.

German and Czechoslovakian tanks: B.T. White, German Tanks and Armoured Vehicles, 1914-1945, London: Ian Allan, 1966; F.M. von Senger und Etterlin, German Tanks of World War II. The Complete Illustrated History of German Armored Fighting Vehicles 1926-1945, J. Lucas, trans., London.: Arms and Armor, 1969; Walter J. Spielberger, Panzer IV and Its Variants, Edward Force, tr., Atglen, PA: Schiffer, 1993; Walter J. Spielberger, Tiger and King Tiger Tanks and their Variants, Sparkford, England: Haynes, 1991; Walter J. Spielberger, Der Panzerkampfwagen Panther und seine Arbarten, Stuttgart: Motorbuch, 1994; Charles K. Kliment and Vladimir Francev, Czechoslovak Armored Fighting Vehicles, 1918-1948, Schiffer, 2004; Bruce Oliver Newsome, The Tiger Tank and Allied Intelligence, Volume IV, Capabilities and Performance, Tank Archives Press, 2020.

Russian and Soviet tanks: John Milsom, Russian Tanks, 1900-1970: The Complete Illustrated History of Soviet Armored Theory and Design, London: Arms & Armour, 1970; Wolfgang Fleischer, Russian Tanks and Armored Vehicles, 1917-1945: An Illustrated Reference, Atglen, PA: Schiffer, 1999; Mikhail Baryatinsky, The IS Tanks. Horsham, Surrey: Ian Allan Publishing, 2006; Neil Stokes, KV Technical History & Variants, Mississauga, Ontario: Air Connection Hobby, 2010; James Kinnear and Yuri Pasholok, T-60 Small Tank and Variants, Stockholm, Sweden: Canfora Publishing, 2017; James Kinnear and Stephen L. Sewell, Soviet T-10 Heavy Tank and Variants, New York: Osprey, 2017; Wolfgang Fleischer, T34: An Illustrated History of Stalin's Greatest Tank, Barnsley, England: Greenhill, 2020.

REFERENCES

Alexander, Arthur J. (1976). Armor Development in the Soviet Union and the United States, Santa Monica, CA: RAND, R-1860-NA.

Anonymous (1942). Britain's Modern Army Illustrated, London: Odhams Press.

Bacon, Reginald (1940). From 1900 Onward, London: Hutchinson.

Beale, Peter (1998). Death by Design: The Fate of British Tank Crews in the Second World War, Stroud, England: Sutton Publishing.

Bond, Brian (1980). British Military Policy Between the Two World Wars, Oxford University Press.

Butler, R.P. (1926). "The Tank Museum: Chapter 3: Little Willie and Mother," The Royal Tank Corps Journal: 3-5.

Cameron, Robert S. (2008). Mobility, Shock, and Firepower: The Emergence of the US Army's Armor Branch, 1917-1945, Washington, DC: Center of Military History, Department of the Army, 2008.

Cappellano, Filippo, and Pier Paolo Battistelli (2012a). Italian Light Tanks, 1919-1945, New Vanguard 191, Oxford, England: Osprey.

- (2012b). Italian Medium Tanks, 1939-1945, New Vanguard 195, Oxford: Osprey, 2012b.

Chamberlain, Peter, and Chris Ellis (1972). Pictorial History of Tanks of the World, 1915-1945, Harrisburg, PA: Stackpole.

Chant, Chris, & Richard Jones (2004). Tanks, St. Paul, Minnesota: Zenith.

Churchill, Winston (1949). The Second World War, Volume 2, Their Finest Hour, London: Cassell.

Drake, C.B. (1919). Report of the Chief of the Motor Transport Corps to the Secretary of War, Washington: Government Printing Office.

Edgerton, David (2005. Warfare State: Britain, 1920-1970, Cambridge University Press.

- (2011). Britain's War Machine: Weapons, Resources, and Experts in the Second World War, London: Allen Lane.

Eisenhower, John D. (2012). "George S. Patton, Jr.", American Heritage, 6/2: 26-33.

Ellis, John (1990). Brute Force: Allied Strategy and Tactics in the Second World War, New York: Viking.

- (1993). The Sharp End: The Fighting Man in World War II, London: Pimlico.

Ellis, Chris, and Denis Bishop (1971). Military Transport of World War I, Poole, England: Blandford.

Ellis, Chris, and Peter Chamberlain (1972). Fighting Vehicles, London: Hamlyn.

- (1975). The Great Tanks, London: Hamlyn.

Ffoulkes, Charles (1940). The Tank and Its Predecessors, Journal of the Society for Army Historical Research, 19/74: 91-98.

Fletcher, David (1991). Mechanised Force: British Tanks Between the Wars, London: HMSO.

Ford, Brian J. (2011). Secret Weapons: Technology, Science and the Race to Win Worrld War II. Oxford, England: Osprey.

Fuller, J.F.C. (1920). Tanks in the Great War, 1914-1918, London: John Murray.

- (1935). The Army in My Time, London: Rich & Cowan.

- (1936). Memoirs of an Unconventional Soldier, London: Ivor Nicholson & Watson Limited.

- (1937). Towards Armageddon: The Defence Problem and its Solution, London: Lovat Dickson.

- (1943). Armored Warfare: An Annotated Edition of Lectureson FSR III, Harrisburg, Pennsylvania: Military Service Publishing Company.

Gibbs, Philip (1946). The Pageant of the Years: An Autobiography, London: William Heinemann.

Gorman, J.T. (1941). The Story of the Tanks, London: Collins.

Gray, Colin S. (2012). War, Peace and International Relations: An Introduction to Strategic History, 2nd Edition, London: Routledge.

Greenhalgh, Elizabeth (2000). "Technology Development in Coalition: The Case of the First World War Tank," The International History Review, 22/4: 806-836.

Harris, J. Paul (1995). Men, Ideas and Tanks: British Military Thought and Armoured Forces, 1903-1939, Manchester University Press.

Hofmann, George F. (1999). "Army Doctrine and the Christie Tank: Failing to Exploit the Operational Level of War," in George F. Hofmann and Donn A. Starry, eds., Camp Colt to Desert Storm: The History of US Armored Forces, Lexington, KY: University Press of Kentucky: 92-143.

Holland, James (2015). The War in the West: A New History, Volume I, Germany Ascendant, 1939-1941, London: Bantam Press.

Hundleby, Maxwell, and Rainer Strasheim (1990). The German A7V Tank and the Captured British Mark IV Tanks of the First World War, Sparkford, England: Foulis/Haynes.

Icks, Robert J. (October 1929). "The Renault Tank," The Royal Tank Corps Journal.

Jentz, Thomas L. (1996). Panzertruppen: The Complete Guide to the Creation and Combat Employment of Germany's Tank Force, 1933-1942, 2 volumes, Atglen, PA: Schiffer.

Johnson, David E. (2003). Fast Tanks and Heavy Bombers: Innovation in the U.S. Army, 1917-1945, Ithaca, NY: Cornell University Press.

Jones, Jr., Wilbur D. (1999). Arming the Eagle: A History of US Weapons Acquisition Since 1775, Fort Belvoir, VA: Defense Systems Management College Press.

Kenez, Peter (1977). Civil War in South Russia, 1919-1920, Berkeley: University of California Press.

Liddell Bart, Basil (1932). War and Western Civilization, 1832-1932: A Study of War as a Political Instrument and the Expression of Mass Democracy, London: Duckworth.

- (1933). "The Mechanisation of War," in: The Interparliamentary Union, ed., What Would be the Character of a New War? London: Victor Gollancz: 49-95.

- (1941). The Current of War, London: Hutchinson.

Lloyd George, David (1938). War Memoirs of David Lloyd George, London: Odhams Press.

Low, Archibald M. (1941). Tanks, London: Hutchinson.

Macksey, Kenneth, and John H. Batchelor (1970). Tank: A History of the Armoured Fighting Vehicle, New York: Charles Scribner's Sons.

Maiolo, Joe (2010). Cry Havoc: The Arms Race and the Second World War, 1931-1941, London: John Murray.

Marshall-Cornwall, James H. (1984). Wars and Rumours of Wars: A Memoir, London: Leo Cooper, Secker & Warburg.

Martel, Giffard le Quesne (1945). Our Armoured Forces, London: Faber & Faber.

Mearsheimer, John (1988). Liddell Hart and the Weight of History, Ithaca: Cornell University Press.

Mitcham, Samuel W. (2007). The Panzer Legions: A Guide to the German Army Tank Divisions of World War II and Their Commanders, Mechanicsburg, PA: Stackpole.

Millett, Allan R., Williamson Murray, and Kenneth H. Watman (1988). "The Effectiveness of Military Organizations," in Allan R. Millett and Williamson Murray, eds., Military Effectiveness, Vol. 1, The First World War, Boston: Allen and Unwin: 1-30.

Mudie, T.C. (September 1927). "Possible Future Developments of Armoured Mechanical Vehicles and their Effect on Tactics," Royal Tank Corps Journal, 8/1: 140-142.

Neame, Philip (1947). Playing with Strife: The Autobiography of a Soldier, London: George G. Harrap.

Ness, Leland S. (2002). Jane's World War II Tanks and Fighting Vehicles: The Complete Guide, London: Harper Collins.

Newsome, Bruce Oliver (2016). Valentine Infantry Tank, 1938-45, Oxford: Osprey.

Newsome, Bruce Oliver, ed., (2020a). PzKw. VI Tiger Tank: The Official Wartime Reports: Coronado, CA: Tank Archives Press.

Newsome, Bruce Oliver (2020b). The Tiger Tank and Allied Intelligence, 4 volumes, Coronado, CA: Tank Archives Press.

Ogorkiewicz, Richard M. (1970). Armoured Forces: A History of Armoured Forces and their Vehicles, New York: Arco.

Orlemann, Eric C., and Keith Haddock (2001). Classic Caterpillar Crawlers, Osceola, Wisconsin: Motorbooks International.

Peck, S. Capel. (October 1929). "The evolution of armoured fighting vehicles," The Royal Tank Corps Journal, 11/2: 204-206.

- (August 1946). "The Early Days of Mechanization," Royal United Services Institution Journal, 91/563: 387-395

Perrett, Bryan (1995). Iron Fist: Classic Armoured Warfare, London: Cassell.

Portway, Donald (1940). Military Science Today, Oxford University Press.

Pullen, Richard (2007). The Landships of Lincoln, 2nd edition, Heighington, England: Tucann.

Rainey, James W. (1983). "Ambivalent Warfare: The Tactical Doctrine of the AEF in World War I," Parameters, 8/3: 34-46.

Rigby, William (1919). Notes for lecture at the Free Trade Hall, Manchester, November 1919, in RACTM Tanks World War I.

Risch, Erna (1989). Quartermaster Support of the Army; A History of the Quartermaster Corps 1775 to 1939, Washington: Center of Military History.

Ross, Gordon MacLeod (1976). The Business of Tanks, 1933 to 1945, Ilfracombe: Arthur H. Stockwell.

Shaw, G.C. (1938). Supply in Modern War, London: Faber & Faber.

Sheppard, E. W. (1938). Tanks in the Next War, The Next War Series, edited by Liddell Hart, London: Geoffrey Bles.

Simpkin, Richard E. (1979). Tank Warfare: An Analysis of Soviet and NATO Tank Philosophy, London: Brasseys.

Speidel, Wilhelm (1949). "The Reichswehr and Soviet Russia," in Donald S. Detwiler, ed., World War II German Military Studies, New York: Garland Publishing, 1979, Vol. 23, Part 10: pp. 1-151.

Stern, Albert (1919). Tanks, 1914-1918: The Logbook of a Pioneer, London: Hodder & Stoughton.

Swinton, Ernest D. (1932). Eyewitness: Being Personal Reminiscences of Certain Phases of the Great War, including the Genesis of the Tank, London: Hodder & Stoughton.

Tooze, Adam (2006). The Wages of Destruction: The Making and Breaking of the Nazi Economy, New York: Viking.

Tucker, Spencer C. (2004). Tanks: An Illustrated History of their Impact, Santa Barbara, CA: ABC-CLIO.

US ASF (United States Army Service Forces) (1948). Logistics in World War II: Final Report of the Army Service Forces: A Report to the Under Secretary of War and the Chief of Staff by the Director of the Service, Supply, & Procurement Division, War Department General Staff, Washington, DC: US GPO

Wells, H.G. (December 1903). "The Land Ironclads," The Strand Magazine, 26/156: 751-64.

Williams-Ellis, Clough, and Amabel Williams Ellis (1919). The Tank Corps, New York: George H. Doran.

Wilson, Dale E. (1988), "The American Expeditionary Forces Tank Corps in World War I: From Creation to Combat," MA Thesis, Temple University, Philadelphia, PA.

- (1999). "World War I: The Birth of American Armor," in George F. Hofmann and Donn A. Starry, eds., Camp Colt to Desert Storm: The History of US Armored Forces, Lexington, KY: University Press of Kentucky: 1-36.

Wilson, Henry Maitland (1950). Eight Years Overseas, 1939-1947, London: Hutchinson.

Wright, Patrick (2000). Tank: The Progress of a Monstrous War Machine, New York: Viking.